THE
DUMB
BOOK

THE DUMB BOOK

**Silly Stories, Stupid People,
and Mega Mistakes
That Crack Us Up**

FROM THE EDITORS OF

Reader's
digest

The Reader's Digest Association, Inc. • New York, NY/Montreal

A READER'S DIGEST BOOK

Library of Congress Cataloging-in-Publication Data is available on request.

ISBN 978-1-62145-138-9

Cover design: George McKeon
Illustrations: H. Caldwell Tanner

We are committed to both the quality of our products and the service we provide
to our customers. We value your comments, so please feel free to contact us.

   The Reader's Digest Association, Inc.
   Adult Trade Publishing
   44 South Broadway
   White Plains, NY 10601

For more Reader's Digest products and information, visit our website:
   www.rd.com (in the United States)
   www.readersdigest.ca (in Canada)

Printed in the United States of America

1 3 5 7 9 10 8 6 4 2

CONTENTS

Introduction

THE GOLDEN AGE OF DUMB

Dumb has always been with us.

But these days—our days—are dumb in ways we never imagined, at levels we never dreamed possible.

Once upon a time, you could get up, have breakfast, go to work, come home, have dinner and go to bed, and experience no dumb that didn't happen to you personally.

Maybe you'd hear a dumb tale or two around the water cooler or see something silly on the evening news. But for the most part, dumb kept its distance. If you wanted some, you had to provide it for yourself or get it from your friends and neighbors—just as you once had to haul your own water and grow your own food.

But today, you can get more dumb in between your first two cups of coffee than your grandparents saw in a lifetime.

You can get it from every corner of the globe, any minute of the day. You don't even need to get out of bed, much less talk to another human being. All you need is a cell phone and an Internet connection to meet:

- *The woman who called 911 because her local McDonald's was out of McNuggets.*

- *The school officials who removed the dictionary from classrooms because of "offensive" material.*

- *The drunk who fell onto the New York City subway tracks and won a $2.3 million settlement.*

- *The Facebooker who cheerfully reminded her friends: "There is no 'i' in happyness!"*

Experts agree: the combination of multibillion-dollar information age technology and the public's apparently insatiable appetite for stupid have brought us into what appears to be a Golden Age of Dumb. Dumb can soar across oceans, rise above mountains, and fly into outer space and back again. Unconstrained by national borders, unbound by language, dumb needs no passport and frequently no translator. On the wings of the Internet, fueled by cell phone cameras and social networking sites, dumb has gone global. It is rapidly replacing love as the international language.

It is a moment unmatched in human history—a feast of foolishness our ancestors could only dream of.

DUMB IN HISTORY:
A Precious Resource, Carefully Guarded

Dumb wasn't always so easy to find. Until very recently, it was carefully shrouded in secrecy and shame. People who did dumb things didn't tell anyone. They took great pains to deny dumb's existence.

We have some nuggets of dumb from the past, of course. We know that:

- *In ancient times, when the legendary general Hannibal lead his army across the Alps to invade Rome, he triggered a massive avalanche by angrily stabbing a snowdrift with his cane. Thousands of soldiers and animals were swept away, and it took his army four days to dig itself out.*

- *Another military legend, General George Custer, had the option of bringing a battery of rapid-fire guns with him to the ill-fated Battle of Little Bighorn. He left them behind, thinking they would slow him down. Custer and his men ended up being cut to ribbons by Sioux warriors.*

- *In 1876, the Western Union telegraph company had a chance to buy the patent for the telephone from Alexander Graham Bell for $100,000—and passed. "While it is a very interesting novelty," said Western Union's William Orton, "it has no commercial possibilities."*

- *In 1962, Decca Records had a chance to sign an up-and-coming pop act, but executive Dick Rowe turned them down. "We don't like your boys' sound." Rowe told their manager. "Groups with guitars particularly are on their way out."*

Proven tales like these are the exception, not the rule. For centuries, most real examples of actual human stupidity have been confined to the privacy of our homes and work places.

To fill the void, humans were forced to produce countless legends of imaginary dumb and circulate them by word of mouth—like the story about the old woman who killed her dog by trying to dry it in the microwave, or the kid who blew up his stomach by mixing Pop Rocks candy and soda.

But in the Internet age, that kind of myth-making is no longer necessary. Huge troves of real, verifiable dumb are now available to anyone and everyone. Who needs legends when we have:

- *A man who mistakenly splashes himself with gasoline—and then lights up the last cigarette he'd ever smoke.*

- *A lawyer who falls to his death through a plate glass window while demonstrating the safety of plate glass windows.*

- *A motorcyclist taking part in a ride to protest helmet laws who flips his bike and dies because he wasn't wearing a helmet. "He would have wanted it that way," said his brother.*

Dumb bosses, dumb workers, dumb celebrities, dumb lawyers, dumb inventors, dumb criminals, dumb bureaucrats, dumb politicians—no more do they dumb in private. Their mistakes can be instantly exposed for all to see by an army of people filming, e-mailing, Facebooking and tweeting about them. Countless websites publish their stories. Countless readers share these tales with their friends and family. We have ever-new ways to see dumb, to be dumb, and to share dumb. Dumb can come at us faster, harder, and in greater volume than ever.

This should be, oddly enough, good news.

Dumb, scientists know, is a critical natural resource, essential to the development and preservation of the species. We depend on dumb. There is no smart without it.

Think about it: somewhere in the murky past is a moment where one caveman saw his hungry neighbor rashly pop a strange toadstool into his mouth. Upon observing his neighbor's subsequent convulsions and painful end, this ancestor concluded that such toadstools would be best left alone.

That means his unfortunate friend did not die dumb in vain. The late lamented helped bring smarts to countless humans who learned from his example and stayed away from the killer mushrooms. Dumb is useful because it teaches us what not to do.

WE NEED DUMB

So it's natural that we're fascinated with dumb. We don't just like it. We need it. Dumb is and has always been essential to the survival of the human race. And thus we find it irresistible. When we see it, we want to share it, and we generally cannot be stopped from doing so.

Humans can't get enough dumb.

And dumb couldn't be happier about it.

Dumb, it turns out, is not a finite resource like oil and gas. Nor is it just a renewable resource like solar or wind power. Dumb is actually a living, self-replicating thing that feeds on attention and grows like kudzu.

All it takes is one video of a kid lighting his shoes on fire by riding a burning skateboard to send thousands—if not millions—of young people worldwide out into the streets armed with matches, lighter fluid, and cell-phone cameras.

So dumb is no longer isolated in fragments. Instead, every available molecule of dumb can now be released into the atmosphere to form powerful new superstructures of stupid.

DUMB GOES NUCLEAR

This phenomenon—scientists call it "dumb fusion," or nuclear dumb—has an incredible, transformative power.

Take, for example, the humble trampoline. Your parents and grandparents saw trampolines as simple backyard toys. Sure, every neighborhood had one kid who did something dumb on one and ended up with a broken arm. But only a few people—mostly personal-injury lawyers—knew exactly how dumb things could get.

And then came YouTube.

In just a few short years, the trampoline was transformed from an innocent toy into a gateway to the Dumb Dimension. If you doubt it, get online and search "trampoline fail" and you will see countless videos featuring people jumping off of roofs onto trampolines, using them to try to dunk basketballs and dive into pools, subjecting themselves to all sorts of pain and injury.

The science of dumb suggests that this widespread trampoline abuse should have a positive outcome. As information about the dangers of trampolines spreads, the theory suggests, humans should come to treat them with caution.

But—to the shock of dumb experts everywhere—something entirely different is happening: trampoline sales are soaring. The industry says its products are more popular than ever before. Instead of fizzling out, the stupid has gone nuclear.

This is a result that science never predicted, and experts are beginning to wonder if we have not reached some sort of essential tipping point.

Is it possible that instead of teaching us how to be smart, dumb is teaching us to become even dumber?

THE DARK SIDE OF DUMB

This is, to be frank, a dangerous situation. As much as we love dumb, it doesn't always love us back. Dropping your phone in the toilet is dumb. Dropping your hair dryer in the tub could be deadly.

But the encouraging news is that even in this Golden Age of Dumb, the survival instinct in humans remains a mighty force.

If you need proof, consider the ultimate test. On at least seven occasions, humans have come *this close* to starting a nuclear war that would render the planet uninhabitable. But no one has pushed the button. And it's a good thing too. Among the events that nearly triggered the war that would have ended life as we know it:

- *A flock of swans*

- *A bear climbing a fence*

- *Faulty chips and glitchy software*

- *The northern lights*

Destroying our planet over any one of those would have been pretty dumb, right? Luckily, we backed off. Our collective smarts kicked in just in time. We've been dumb—but not that dumb.

So welcome to the *The Dumb Book*. It will serve as your guide to dumb in all of its historic and modern forms. When you have finished this book, you will have everything you need to be as dumb as you want. And hopefully, you'll be a little smarter for it.

DUMB
BOSSES

**They're the six words that strike
fear into any worker's heart:**

"THE BOSS WANTS TO SEE YOU."

It doesn't have to be a disaster. You could be in line for praise, a raise, or even a promotion. But as you take that long slow walk down the cubicle aisle to the corner office, you know it's much more likely that you're about to get yelled at.

And when a boss is yelling, can the dark shadow of Big Dumb be far away?

After all, based on what our readers tell us, we live in a world where:

You might get fired for wearing a Green Bay Packers tie.

You might be reprimanded for looking down on a boss who's six inches shorter than you.

You might be getting set up so that the boss's girlfriend's angry, jilted husband beats you up instead of him.

The bad news is that stuff like that happens to us all the time.

The good news is that when it does, we can't wait to talk about it. Our unscientific survey here at Reader's Digest shows that for every story about a dumb celebrity or dumb husband or dumb bureaucrat, there are approximately 432.7 stories about dumb bosses.

Boss Dumb is, in a word, special. It's not that it's fundamentally different from other kinds of stupid. Bosses are dumb just like everybody else; they're overworked or misinformed or behind the times or wrapped up in dumb rules handed down by their own dumb bosses.

No, what makes Boss Dumb so fascinating is that the boss has *power*. The boss rules our lives. When somebody sitting next to you on the bus does something dumb, it's of passing interest. When your boss does something dumb, it can change your world.

And while many of us are blessed with bosses who treat us well, we all know that inside every boss lurks a ruthless dictator. Somehow they all eventually learn to think like baseball's Gene Mauch, the dugout boss who once said: "I'm not the manager because I'm always right, but I'm always right because I'm the manager."

In fact, bosses are a uniquely nasty bunch. Rainn Wilson, who is considered by some to be a leading expert on the subject by playing the egomaniacal Dwight Schrute on TV's *The Office,* described the boss mentality this way:

> *Bond villains are a great source of inspiration for me. At their desks you'll often find a sequence of buttons, the sole purpose of which is behavioral correction. Any modern manager will thrive with one of those fear-the-boss workstations.*

So the boss is out to get you; there's just no doubt about it. It's their nature and they can't help themselves.

But if power corrupts, it also, apparently, stupefies. A boss may be powerful, but he's bound to be dumb eventually.

Keep that in mind if—make that *when*—you're a boss. Because you know that in your heart of hearts, you want to be one.

"I do! I do! But I won't be dumb!" you say. "My people will love me! I'll be nice! I'll be smart! I'll be the smartest boss ever!"

Sure you will, boss. Sure you will.

Working for the Man

Working for a big corporation, you can feel pretty unimportant. In fact, you can begin to wonder exactly how much anybody cares about what you're doing.

So a colleague and I decided to test the water. He would stop working, and I would work like never before.

At the end of our test period, we had a performance review. His said: "Worked well and was barely noticeable. Two thumbs up!"

Mine said, "Overall negative impression," and recommended that I study my friend's work habits. He got a raise, and I didn't.

—TALES OF CORPORATE OPPRESSION, CORPORATEOPPRESSION.COM

Even a working man's hero like Willie Nelson can tap his inner boss when he needs to. His longtime harmonica player, Mickey Raphael, says working for Willie was great but getting paid took a little while.

"I just decided to follow him around Texas and show up wherever they were playing," Raphael once recalled.

"And at one of them, Willie asked Paul English, the drummer and leader of the band, 'What are we paying Mickey?'

"Paul said, 'Nothing, he just showed up.' Willie said, 'Well, double his salary.'"

—SOURCE: RIVERREPORTER.COM

Today I asked my bosses for three weeks off in July to go on a much-needed vacation. Their response was to fire me on the spot. The punch line: my bosses are my aunt and uncle. FML.

—FMYLIFE.COM

Our company chairman was famous for burning through assistants. One was a young man whose name was Alan, but the chairman called him "Seven." For days after being hired, Alan endured the chairman yelling down the hall, "Seven! Seven!"

Finally, Alan asked, "Why do you call me Seven?"

"Because you're the seventh assistant I've hired this month," the chairman answered.

Alan got it but kindly asked, "Why don't you just call me by my name?"

"Because you're not going to be around @#$# long enough for me to learn your #$%@# name!" the chairman replied. He then pushed passed Alan, shouting to his other assistant, "Kate! Get rid of Seven and get me Eight!"

—TALES OF CORPORATE OPPRESSION, CORPORATEOPPRESSION.COM

As a teenager, I worked at a diner that had an all-glass front. One day, a blizzard blew in, knocking the wind chill factor down to 40 below. But my boss sent me outside anyway to wash the windows.

"Put some alcohol in that bucket so the water doesn't freeze," he said.

"The water? What about me?" I asked.

He grunted, "You're too young for alcohol."

—SCOTT DONOVAN

After I'd been working in a small marketing agency for two years, my boss called me into his office one afternoon and told me I was finally receiving a promotion and a raise. I was elated. But when I reminded him about it the next day, he changed his tune. I started to argue, but he cut me off.

"You know better than to take me seriously in the afternoons," he said. "I'm drunk every afternoon."

—ELIZABETH B.

Some people are so sensitive. My boss just chewed me out because, according to him, I look down on him. I'm six foot five. FML.

—FMYLIFE.COM

It's Good to Be The Boss

It's good to be the boss—until you screw up and everyone can see it. That's what happened to Captain Francesco Schettino of the ill-fated *Costa Concordia,* the cruise ship that ran aground in Italy on his watch in 2012. Not only is Schettino accused of sailing too close to shore, he allegedly fled the sinking ship long before the rest of the passengers and crew.

Schettino has defended his actions, saying he tripped and accidentally fell in the lifeboat. A trial in Italy will reveal the truth, but the whole incident left more than one observer recalling the words attributed to the late British prime minister Winston Churchill: "There are three things I like about Italian ships. First, their cuisine, which is unsurpassed. Second, their service, which is quite superb. And then, in time of emergency, there is none of this nonsense about women and children first."

"Ex-NBC Exec Gets Chair"

—THE MIAMI HERALD

Our former department head was famous for his malaprops. Here are his greatest hits:

- *The Greek pyramids weren't built in a day.*

- *Spurt me out an e-mail.*

- *Let's not put the horse before the cart.*

- *Tonight we're eating at the Tibetian restaurant.*

- *It's not rocket surgery.*

- *It's all smoke and windows.*

- *Nothing is nailed in stone.*

- *Sometimes you have to roll the dice, and it comes up tails.*

—STEVE WEHMOFF

I've been running a bar in Prague for many years, and I live in the same building. I happen to be a sleepwalker, and after one episode, I woke up naked on the roof, locked out of my own apartment. The only thing I could find in the attic to wear was an ancient, filthy, rubber raincoat.

Out of options, I put it on, went downstairs to my bar, knocked on the back window, and asked Jana, the cleaner, to let me in. She looked at me in horror. "Don't ask," I said. But soon enough, I was sitting at the bar, waiting for a friend with some keys, shaking out the cobwebs, and having a drink.

Unfortunately, my friend was slow to arrive, but my drinks weren't. Soon enough customers were asking the bartender, "Who's the strange drunk naked guy in the too-small, grease-smeared, black rubber raincoat down at the end of the bar?"

"Oh, don't mind him," he said. "That's the owner!"

—GLEN EMERY

I'd gone on vacation without having processed a pay raise for one of the employees of our medical practice. When I returned, I discovered that my boss had filed the forms away. I opened the file cabinet and looked up the employee's last name, first name, subject matter—nothing.

"Hey, where did you file those papers?" I asked my boss.

"Look under *M*," he said.

"M?" I asked. "But his initials are *C. S.* Why would you file it under *M*?"

Exasperated, he said, "For money."

—DEBORAH BUSH

While on the job, I was unpleasantly surprised by the early arrival of my monthly cycle. After unsuccessfully begging every woman I could for "logistical support," I reluctantly approached my supervisor, Jerry, and, choosing my words carefully, stammered, "I . . . um . . . would like to request permission to go home. I am . . . having trouble with . . . a female issue that . . . I'm not able to successfully resolve."

"Sure, no problem," said Jerry. "But tell me, which female?"

—GLENDA HERRIN

Once after work, my boss, a self-titled "e-mail man," sent me a text message instructing me to check my e-mail. I rushed over to my computer and pulled up the important missive. It contained two words: "Call me."

—MARTIN HOFFMANN

One night I worked late with my boss fielding customer requests. It was a quiet, unremarkable evening until one call left him with a look of horror on his face. Turns out he'd been making some questionable decisions in his personal life and was about to pay the price.

"I have to get out of here!" he yelled. "That was my girlfriend. Her husband just found out about me. He's on his way over here right now!"

The husband had never laid eyes on him, he said, but knew he worked late nights. My boss bolted out the door but not before telling me, "Keep answering those phone calls!"

Being eager to please, I stayed put. But then it hit me: my boss was setting me up. He was hoping I'd be mistaken for the boyfriend!

I quickly grabbed my coat, turned out the lights, and got out of there.

—PHIL P.

Does anything sound dumber than a boss trying to save a few bucks? *Inc.* magazine collected these quotes from employee performance reviews, most of which would seem to suggest that someone besides the employee needs a review:

- *"I know you are my best employee and you train all our new employees. However, I don't see how that qualifies you for a raise."*

- *"That's right, no raise this year. Maybe next year when you come off that high horse, you'll get my coffee when I ask you to."*

- *"Before you came to my department, you were such a shining star—full of new ideas and enthusiasm. What happened to you?"*

How Did They Get to the Top of the Ladder?

Another boss who found himself pinned in the harsh glare of the dumb-cam is Roger Goodell, Commissioner of the National Football League, who hired replacement referees to deal with the league's labor problem.

The result was chaos—a string of notably awful on-field calls and embarrassing confusion, playing out on national television and triggering an avalanche of withering criticism.

And on Twitter and late-night television, the nation's comics had a field day:

- *Breaking sports news: NFL refs just reviewed '86 World Series. Bill Buckner did NOT drop the ball.*

- *You know what would be funny? If the Olympic refs went on strike and someone from real estate had to judge diving.*

- *Replacement refs are God's judgment for not respecting his holy day.*

- *Fans say they're fed up with these phony refs and they want them back where they belong, in the NBA.*

- *BREAKING: Referee lockout to end; replacement refs to report back to Foot Locker ASAP.*

At my old office, one of the bosses went crazy and threw his computer out the window, 50 floors up. Thankfully, no one was hurt—it bounced on a ledge a few stories down and stayed there. Later, the boss was taken out of the office in a straitjacket. Oddly enough, he returned to work a month later.

—B. O.

"Four More Newspapers Switch to Offset: Conversion Is Not Always Soomth"

—KANSAS PUBLISHER

I was working as a reporter for an "alternative" New York City newspaper. Our office was a storefront with a double door. The publisher owned a small Honda, a tiny 1970s model no bigger than a shopping cart. Or so it seemed, until he decided to park it in the office at night to avoid the hassle of parking on the street.

"It will never fit," we told him.

"Sure it will," he said.

So we pushed all the desks against the wall, and he backed the vehicle across the sidewalk. Sure enough, the rear end of the car made it through the door with an inch to spare on either side. Wow! This was actually going to work! We were going to park a car in the middle of our office!

Alas, no. Half an hour later, and dizzy from breathing carbon monoxide, he could not squeeze the side mirrors through the doors. The strange thing is, as we moved our desks back, I was as disappointed as my boss that his scheme didn't work.

—D. N.

It was a typical hectic Friday afternoon at our law office. My boss, meanwhile, was hundreds of miles away at a luxury resort, preparing for a meeting. In the midst of my insane day, I got an urgent call from him.

"You have to phone the hotel right away. It's important," my boss said. "Ask them to send someone to the pool area immediately."

"What's wrong?" I asked.

"We haven't seen a waiter in 20 minutes, and we need our drinks refreshed."

—BONAH BACHENHEIMER

The front office asked us to figure out the square footage dedicated to each department in our clothing store. To save time, I suggested we count the ceiling tiles above each department.

"They're each two square feet. Counting the tiles would give us an accurate dimension of each department without having to work around all the displays," I explained.

My boss hated the idea. "Hell-ooo," she said, sarcastically. "We need the square footage of the floor, not the ceiling."

—TERRI HANKE

After I worked through lunch to help my boss with a report, he offered to show his appreciation by taking me out for a bite. The place he had in mind had a wonderful buffet, he said, with foods from around the world. I was absolutely salivating with each detail. So what was his idea of an exotic dining establishment? Sam's Club. We spent the hour dining on the free samples they handed out.

—WENDY BROWN

My boss's biggest nemesis is the English language. During one meeting, I asked about the status of a particular report. He replied, "We aren't going to prepare that report. It would be an exercise in fertility."

It would be funnier if he didn't earn four times more than I do.

—SUE T.

On my first day at a new job, I arrived to find someone in the office that I'd been told would be mine. Puzzled, I went to find the person who had hired me, but she was away at a conference. So I told another person my story. She made a few calls, then told me to find a place to sit.

"Don't speak to anyone," she ordered. "Just wait for someone to find you something to do until your boss returns."

Turns out, my boss had forgotten to fire the person I was replacing before she left town.

—NANCY E.

My boss was a real gentleman. Although it wasn't my job, he once made me mow the lawn around our office building. I was wearing a dress and high heels.

—TAMARA T.

My boss was notoriously cheap, so when he handed me a birthday card, I was pleasantly surprised.

"Thank you," I said.

"You're welcome," he replied. "And when you get through reading it, take it to Robin down the hall. It's her birthday today too."

—GAIL SNYDER

DUMB BOSSES

As an employee representative, it was my unfortunate duty to do battle with our boss whenever he asked too much of his employees.

"You think you know everything, don't you?" he yelled at me once.

"No, sir, I don't," I countered. "But I do know what the law says. And the law says—"

"The law!?" he roared. "The law has absolutely nothing to do with what goes on in this company!"

—Y. F.

I was performing with another comic, and part of our deal was a free meal. After my set, I asked our waitress if I could get a bite. She said no. That's not usually how it works, so I asked to speak with the manager.

Next thing I knew, he was charging straight at me, screaming that I was rude to his waitress. He chased me around the table, yelling and lunging at me. Thankfully, the bouncer separated us.

When the other comic got offstage, I said, "You won't believe this, but the manager tried to kill me!"

"Really?" he said. "I didn't think your set was that bad."

—D. F. SWEEDLER

I was five-and-a-half-months pregnant, and the principal decided it was time we had a chat about dress code . . . my dress code. "I don't know if you are aware, but your body is changing," she said awkwardly. "I'm concerned because your breasts have become inappropriately large for a secondary school teacher."

A long, uncomfortable pause followed. I didn't know what to say. Then she broke the silence. "That's all," she said, dismissing me. She never did say what she expected me to do about the problem.

—KRISTEN J.

My boss likes to save pennies. How much? I caught him in the break room retrieving paper cups from the trash and shoving them back into the dispenser next to the water cooler. He didn't even bother wiping off the lipstick.

—BARBARA B.

During my brother-in-law's first performance review, his boss said, "I'm not quite sure what it is you do here. But, whatever it is, could you do it faster?"

—JEANIE WAARA

Bosses in the News:

- *A New Zealand office worker was axed for using bold uppercase letters in an e-mail to coworkers on how to properly fill out forms. The company deemed the capital letters confrontational.*

- *Wells Fargo fired a customer service representative with seven years on the job after discovering he'd put a cardboard cutout of a dime in a Laundromat washing machine nearly 50 years earlier.*

- *A waiter in Fort Lauderdale, Florida, claims he was let go after leaving his post to help a woman who was being carjacked in the parking lot.*

- *A fashion model was reportedly fired for being too fat. The model is five ten and weighs 120 pounds.*

- *A Chicago car salesman was shown the door for wearing a Green Bay Packers tie to work.*

—READER'S DIGEST

Being a boss means making decisions. And based on the decisions some bosses make, the world needs some better boss schools. As noted in *AdWeek,* each one of these terrible decisions was approved by somebody's boss:

- *During Hurricane Sandy, the Gap tweeted: "All impacted by Sandy, stay safe! We'll be doing lots of shopping at Gap.com today. How about you?" An apology soon followed.*

- *For its billboard in Encinitas, California, Spy Sunglasses chose the slogan, "Happy to Sit on Your Face." The billboard came down in a week.*

- *The tweet team at Nabisco suggested to followers: "Ever bring your own Oreo cookies to the movie theater?" Movie theater owners weren't amused, and AMC Theatres replied: "Not cool, cookie!"*

- *The British fashion brand Harvey Nichols adopted a new slogan that seemed innocent enough: "Try to Contain Your Excitement." However, they chose to illustrate the slogan with pictures of models who'd wet their pants.*

Today I was fired by my boss because of the way I laugh. Apparently, it reminds him too much of his ex-wife's laugh. I'm a guy. FML.

—FMYLIFE.COM

My boss gave the first employee-of-the-month award to himself.

—BOBSUTTON.TYPEPAD.COM

My boss hired a guy who was color-blind to do color corrections at the photo lab. After angry customers returned their pictures, I informed my boss. She told me that I was putting him down to build myself up.

—J@AOL

My editor left a note on a recipe story I was working on. It read, "Please be specific. Do you have to peel the egg before you boil it?"

—FORBES.COM

"2 Producers Quit Show Complaining Report has More Substance then Hype"

—NAPLES (FL) DAILY NEWS

With talk of downsizing the U.S. Postal Service always in the air, our union steward passed the word to all the letter carriers that we needed to be proactive.

"Save our jobs," he urged. "Email your Congressman."

—SUSAN KEMP

DUMB BOSSES

DUMB
WORKERS

WORK **DRIVES US NUTS.**

And along the way, it makes us dumb.

Work, after all, can be boring, frustrating, demanding, stressful—and completely unavoidable. So unless you win the lottery—and even if you do—you'll probably spend most of your life on the job. And once you're there, there's a very good chance that you'll eventually do something stupid:

> *Like the Des Moines pizza delivery man who relieved himself on a light-tipping customer's door.*

> *Like the Kansas City dollar store worker who tried to prank a colleague by putting laxatives in a couple of bottles of Coke—and ended up sending a customer to the hospital.*

> *Like the Wisconsin cemetery worker who stole a fine Telecaster electric guitar from the casket of a vet who wanted to be buried with it. "This isn't something I normally do," said the worker. "I just have a respect for fine musical instruments."*

Most of us don't end up in the headlines, fortunately. But we've all seen something or done something that reminds us that when it comes to dumb, no workplace is safe.

Some say this is no accident. Companies have long been suspected of favoring dumb workers over pricier smart ones. A financial manager from South Carolina recently sued his employers for age discrimination after they claimed to favor hiring of the "young and dumb" over more experienced older workers like himself.

Others, believe that hiring the dumb is almost inevitable because many of our dumbest workers survive by carefully honing interviewing skills. They've read all the job search books and practiced the interview questions. They are good performers until they get the job.

Make no mistake—dumb workers may be cheaper in the short run, but the costs kick in eventually.

And even those of us who aren't naturally dumb can get that way pretty quickly. Workplace distractions like e-mail or chattering colleagues literally stupefy us. According to *The New York Times,* a study from the University of California at Irvine found:

> *"A typical office worker gets only 11 minutes between each interruption, while it takes an average of 25 minutes to return to the original task."*

And another study by an IT professor and a psychologist from Carnegie Mellon University discovered that:

> *"The distraction of an interruption, combined with the brain drain of preparing for that interruption, made our test takers 20 percent dumber."*

So in the age of multitasking, staying smart on the job—or even in the job interview—is an uphill battle. And based on what you'll see in this chapter, it's one that many of us are clearly losing.

But don't fret too much. As the folks at the Bootstrapper blog point out, dumb colleagues can make you look good. "Having a few fools around can raise your perceived value," Bootstrapper wrote. "Yes, your boss really does notice."

All in a Day's Work

At our business, we ask job applicants to fill out a questionnaire before we get to the interview phase. Among the questions: "Choose one word to summarize your strongest professional attribute."

One woman wrote, "I'm very good at following instructions."

—DAVE NICHOLSON

I couldn't find my luggage at the airport baggage area. So I went to the lost luggage office and told the worker there that my bags never showed up.

She smiled and told me not to worry; they were trained professionals, and I was in good hands. "Now," she asked me, "has your plane arrived yet?"

—RINKWORKS.COM

Days after posting a bilingual traffic sign in Swansea, Wales, officials were alerted to a problem. The English half was fine, but the Welsh, which had been e-mailed to the translator and returned minutes later, read, when translated back into English, "I am not in the office."

—*READER'S DIGEST*

Coworker 1: My son just turned 18 months old.

Coworker 2: So is that like a year and a half old?

Coworker 1: You really aren't sure if 18 months is a year and a half?

Coworker 2: How am I supposed to know that? I don't have kids.

—ADAM FREDERICK

My scrupulously honest husband caught a coworker helping herself to company trash bags and called her on it. "So what?" she argued. "They're just going to throw them away."

—PATRICIA HUTCHENS

A good side benefit of training new hires is that it makes us revisit our routine practices and spruce them up. At my restaurant, I recently joined two of our managers showing a new employee around.

"So, what's that brush for?" the new hire asked.

"It's used to clean toilet bowls in the lobby," said the first manager.

"Actually, it's for scrubbing deep fryers," said the second manager.

"Well, I've been cleaning toilets with it," said the first manager.

"Er, I'm putting in for a new brush," said the second manager. "Let's keep quiet about this."

—NOTALWAYSWORKING.COM

I was working the cash register in a deli when a coworker came over with his lunch. "Can you ring me up for two biscuits with the half-off discount and tell me how much it is?" he said. "I rang it up on the calculator, but I don't think it's right."

"Well, what did you get?" I asked.

"I typed in 89¢ times two and then divided it in half, and I ended up with 89¢ again!" he said.

"Really?" I said, pausing to see if the light bulb would go off. It didn't.

"What?" my colleague said.

"What's 89¢ times two, divided by two?"

That did it. "Oh God," he said, embarrassed. "Just ring me up, please."

—NOTALWAYSWORKING.COM

DUMB WORKERS

My boss at the warehouse told the new guy not to stack boxes more than head-high. "If the inspector shows up," he said, "we'd get in trouble. So, questions?"

"Yeah," said the new guy. "How tall is the inspector?"

—CYNTHIA FRANKLIN

One of the less difficult blanks to fill in on our job application is: "Position Wanted." One job seeker wrote "Sitting."

—FLO TRAYWICK

A postal worker in North Carolina recently applied for workers' compensation benefits after allegedly injuring her shoulder on the job, claiming that she could no longer "stand, sit, kneel, squat, climb, bend, reach, or grasp."

Sounds tough—but federal investigators thought it also sounded fishy. Not just because the worker had been seen lifting heavy bags of groceries, and not just because she'd been spotted zip-lining with her husband on a cruise.

What really did her in was becoming a contestant on *The Price is Right*.

According to a federal indictment, the supposedly crippled worker was seen on national television spinning the show's signature "Big Wheel" twice. The first time, the feds said, she "raised her left arm above her head and gripped the handle with her left hand." The second time, she "raised both arms above her head and gripped the same handle with both hands."

The worker pled guilty to fraud. "I've seen every kind of case you can see," one investigator said. "The secret is you've got to have your camera up, when they do what they're doing."

—OPPOSINGVIEWS.COM

An elevator in our office building is frequently out of order. The last time, maintenance posted a sign that summed up the situation: "Elevator Closed for Temporary Repairs."

—TERRI CRUDUP

Outrageous Excuses

Employees will say anything to dodge a day's work, as CareerBuilder revealed in its study of "outrageous excuses" reported by human resource workers:

- *Employee's cat had the hiccups.*

- *Employee got distracted watching the* Today *show.*

- *Employee thought she had won the lottery. (She hadn't.)*

- *Employee's angry roommate cut the cord to his phone charger, so it didn't charge and his alarm didn't go off.*

- *Employee believed his commute time should count toward his work hours.*

- *Employee claimed a fox stole her car keys.*

- *Employee was late because of a job interview with another firm.*

- *Employee's leg was trapped between a subway car and the platform. (Turned out to be true.)*

Sitting at my desk, I heard a colleague on the phone with a customer. "I'm sorry, sir, but we don't cover vehicles outside the United States," he said.

Five minutes later, he had second thoughts.

"I think I told the customer the wrong thing," he said. "Is Hawaii part of the United States?"

—STUPIDCOWORKERS.COM

After Doug, a coworker, complained about the oil stains on his clothes every time he did his laundry, our colleague said the cause was likely the bearings in his washing machine, an expensive repair job. He suggested Doug would be better off buying a new washer.

Doug did just that and hauled his old machine to the dump. He hooked up the new one and put in a load of laundry. But once again, he noticed oil stains on his clothes—when he took them out of the dryer.

—GREGG MITCHELL

"Chick Accuses Some of Her Male Colleagues of Sexism"

—*LOS ANGELES TIMES*

Today during lunch, my coworker offered me her food, claiming she was full. I was still quite hungry, so I gratefully accepted.

She must have been out to get me; halfway through the sandwich, my boss walked in, shouting, "Who took my lunch?" FML.

—FMYLIFE.COM

How to Ace the Job Interview

From the nation's capital, *Washingtonian Magazine* compiled these job interview horror stories:

- *"I was interviewing someone who took a cell phone call and asked me to leave my office while they talked."*

- *"A nervous interviewee came into my office, and in the middle of the handshake he accidentally spit his gum out in my face."*

- *"One interviewee made a West Virginia joke, only to discover [the interviewer] was from West Virginia."*

- *"When a candidate was asked about his greatest accomplishment, he replied that it was writing a short novel. When the interviewer said, 'No, I mean something you did while at work,' the candidate replied, 'But I did write it while at work!'"*

Word to the wise: powerful prescription medication and job hunting don't always mix. While waiting for an interview, I started having an unbearable panic attack. I've had them before and I was prepared—I popped a Klonopin to relax.

It worked—too well. I hadn't counted on my empty stomach magnifying the effect. Soon I was slouching in my chair with a big smile on my face. When I noticed that they'd noticed, I told them exactly what was going on, thinking, "Hey, no big deal. This is going great. Let's keep this rolling."

They weren't so relaxed about it. They thanked me for my time, and showed me the door.

—REDDIT

"First Microbes Breathed Sulfur Before It Was Cool"

—THE WASHINGTON POST

My wife and I were having lunch at a fashionable eatery in Annapolis when we noticed what looked like a familiar face at the next table. Screwing up my courage, I asked, "Excuse me. Aren't you Marlin Fitzwater, the former White House press secretary?"

"Yes, I am," he acknowledged, and graciously interrupted his lunch to talk to us.

As we were leaving the restaurant, I remarked to the hostess, "Do you know you have Marlin Fitzwater on the terrace?"

"I'm not sure about that," she replied, "but we have Perrier and Evian at the bar."

—BRUCE F. HENDERSON

I was preparing to teach a college course on the history of movie censorship and went to the library to take out films that had been censored. "Do you have any banned movies in your collection?" I asked the librarian.

"Oh yes," she answered. "We have some really good ones. What would you like: Tomy Dorsey? Glenn Miller?"

—PAUL H. STACY

The first day at my new health club I asked the girl at the front desk, "I like to exercise after work. What are your hours?"

"Our club is open 24/7," she told me excitedly, "Monday through Saturday."

—APRYL CAVENDER

Watercooler Chat

At the call center where I once worked, we were required to use the customer's name five times, no matter how brief the call.

A friend of mine had a lot of trouble with this, so his team leader decided to coach him, listen to his calls and telling him what he should do differently. The very first call they received was from somebody asking for a service they didn't provide. Here's how my friend solved the problem:

Customer: Do you provide such and such service?

Colleague: Can I get your name, please?

Customer: Sure, it's John.

Colleague: John. John, John, John, John, no, we don't. Thanks for calling.

—TALES OF CORPORATE OPPRESSION, CORPORATEOPPRESSION.COM

The receptionist where I work isn't exactly on top of every detail of company life. One day we heard her announce: "Jim Smith, please come to the office. You have a telephone call."

"You may want to speak up," my colleague said. "Also, if he shows up, I'm getting out of here fast."

"Why, don't you like him?" the receptionist asked.

"No, it's not that at all," my colleague answered. "It's just that he's been dead for over a year."

—STUPIDCOWORKERS.COM

Our colleague, a frequenter of pubs, applied for a vanity license plate that would cement his reputation as the "bar king." A week later he arrived to work with his new plates: BARKING.

—NANCY SEND

We asked prospective job applicants at our business to fill out a questionnaire. For the line "Choose one word to summarize your strongest professional attribute," one woman wrote, "I'm very good at following instructions."

—DAVE NICHOLSON

After a recent move, I made up a list of companies, agencies and services that needed to know my new address and phoned each to ask them to make the change. Everything went smoothly until I made a call to one of my frequent-flier accounts. After I explained to her what I wanted to do, the woman I reached in customer service told me, "I'm sorry; we can't do that over the phone. You will have to fill out our change-of-address form."

"How do I get one of those?" I asked.

"We'd be happy to provide you with one," she said pleasantly. "Can I have your new address so I can mail it to you?"

After booking my 90-year-old mother on a flight from Florida to Nevada, I called the airline to go over her needs. The woman representative listened patiently as I requested a wheelchair and an attendant for my mother because of her arthritis and impaired vision. I also asked for a special meal and assistance in changing planes.

My apprehension lightened a bit when the woman assured me everything would be taken care of. I thanked her profusely.

"Why, you're welcome," she replied. I was about to hang up when she cheerfully asked, "And will your mother be needing a rental car?"

—THOMAS A. CORBETT

There's No Such Thing as a Dumb Question, or Is There?

I work in the toy department at a Walmart, and one day I was asked to do a price check.

The cashier explained that a customer wanted to buy some puzzles, priced at four for $5.00, but they were ringing up at $1.25 apiece.

Apparently neither the customer nor the cashier ever made it through sixth grade math.

—RINKWORKS.COM

We'd just received a new shipment, but as usual the supplier wasn't exactly on top of things.

"They sent us 59 hats in one box, and 13 in the other!" I said.

"What's so strange about that?" my colleague asked.

"The hats are supposed to be packaged in multiples of twelve," I said.

"So what are you complaining about?" he said.

"Fifty-nine in one box, and 13 in the other," I replied. "It doesn't make sense."

"But they're both multiples of twelve!" my colleague said. "What's the problem?"

—NOTALWAYSWORKING.COM

Coworker: "Hey, I see you have Saturday off. Do you mind taking my shift?"

Me: "I can't. My brother is getting married on Saturday."

Coworker: "Do you have to stay for the entire thing?"

—NOTALWAYSWORKING.COM

The human resource experts at Workforce.com rounded up some of the dumbest questions workers ask—and the answers they'd love to deliver:

Q: Can I have my salary deferred until next year so I don't have to pay taxes this year? I don't need the money this year.

A: You may not need the money this year, but the IRS does.

Q: I falsified my résumé. Now that I'm working here, can I change it?

A: Sure. Can we change your employment status?

Q: Can my supervisor require me to have specific working hours?

A: We could waive the requirement if you waive the requirement that we provide a specific paycheck at a specific time.

Q: Can I wear a swimsuit and towel on casual day?

A: It'd be appropriate for taking a dip in the job candidate pool.

Q: Will you give me a raise if I stop smoking marijuana?

A: Sorry. There's no rainbow at the end of this pot.

Q: Since my mother and father both died before I came to work at this company, will I be credited for bereavement leave I didn't have to take?

A: Well, you've apparently been credited with intelligence you don't intend to use, so let's call it even.

Q: Every day my supervisor tells me to stop chatting and get back to work. Can he do that?

A: Yes. Now get back to work.

Before I left town for college, I worked as a shift manager at a fast-food restaurant in Minnesota. One day I had this exchange with one of my staff:

"You're going to Penn State, right?" he asked.

"No, actually I'm going to the University of Pennsylvania," I replied.

"That's what I said."

"The University of Pennsylvania is an entirely different school," I said.

"No, it's not," my coworker said.

"Yes it is," I said. "The University of Pennsylvania is in the Ivy League, and Penn State is in the Big Ten."

"What's the Ivy League?"

"The Ivy League is all of the schools like Harvard, Yale, and Princeton."

"Oh," said my coworker. "I always thought you were a nobody!"

That's when my store manager, who was listening to the entire conversation, turned to my colleague and said:

"Have you ever considered that if he were a nobody, you would be his boss and not the other way around?"

—NOTALWAYSWORKING.COM

DUMB WORKERS

I was training a new hire at our sandwich shop when she asked me about one of the ingredients.

"So, what animal does turkey come from?"

"Turkey," I said.

"Yeah, the turkey breast," she said. "What animal is that from?"

I gave up. "Cow."

"Really?"

"No."

The real punch line is that she became the store manager.

—NOTALWAYSWORKING.COM

I'm in charge of the direct-deposit paperwork for new hires and recently had this exchange:

New Hire: "And here's my direct deposit form."

Me: "Ah, since this is a joint account, you'll have to have your husband sign as well. You can bring this back tomorrow."

New Hire: "Do I have to? I mean, I have the check right here."

Me: "It's a legal document, so yes, he has to sign it."

New Hire: "Can't I just forge it?"

—BLOGLOVIN.COM

The stoplight on the corner buzzes when it's safe to cross the street. A coworker once asked if I knew what the buzzer was for. I explained that it signals to blind people when the light is red.

She responded, appalled, "What on earth are blind people doing driving?"

—RINKWORKS.COM

I'm an emergency medical technician in California, and one day I had to check in an elderly patient at a local hospital.

"What's the birth date of the patient?" the registration clerk said.

"One-five-nineteen nineteen," I said.

"Nineteen what?" asked the clerk

"Nineteen," I said.

"Nineteen WHAT?" the clerk said again.

"Nineteen nineteen," I said.

"That does not make any sense," the clerk said flatly. "Nineteen what? Nineteen ninety, nineteen eighty-five . . . nineteen what?"

"I doubt it was the nineteen nineties," I said, looking at my ninety something patient. "Like I said, nineteen nineteen."

"Nineteen WHAT???" the clerk shouted.

"ONE NINE ONE NINE!" I shouted back.

"Ooooooohhh," said the clerk.

—NOTALWAYSWORKING.COM

Author Jenny Lawson spent fifteen years in human resources, penning a memoir called *Let's Pretend This Never Happened* that makes you worry about the economic future of the nation.

One typical tale: in one two-month stretch, "six separate men filled in the 'sex' blank on their job application with some variation of 'Depends on who's offering,'" Lawson recalled. "Two answered, 'Yes, please,' and one wrote, 'No, thank you.'"

You'd think that all nine applicants would have been disqualified, but you'd be wrong. "I hired the last one because he seemed polite," Lawson wrote.

—SOURCE: THEBLOGGESS.COM

DUMB WORKERS

I remarked to one of my coworkers the other day about how nice it was that we're getting more daylight now.

"It must be all that global warming," she replied.

—STRAIGHTDOPE.COM

A scene from my newspaper, where I sometimes help my coworker design ads:

Coworker: This ad is wrong.

Me: Oh? What's wrong with it?

Coworker: The text looks bad. There's something wrong with it. I don't like it.

Me: Actually, this ad is one you created a month ago. All I did was resize it.

Coworker, after staring at the ad for ten seconds: Oh, you know what? Never mind, this looks good!

—NOTALWAYSWORKING.COM

Coworker No. 1: Listen to this. It's a band from South Africa.

Coworker No. 2: Oh, I like them. But why are they banned from South Africa?

Coworker No. 1: That's just were they're from; they're a band from South Africa.

Coworker No. 2: But why aren't they allowed to play there?

Coworker No. 1: No, they are a band from South Africa. They're not banned from playing there.

Coworker No. 2: Oh! I get it!

Coworker No. 3: Best conversation ever.

—BLOGLOVIN.COM

"Worker Suffers Leg Pain after Crane Drops 800-Pound Ball on His Head"

—ASSOCIATED PRESS

The day after a major storm, the shelves at the supermarket were pretty bare—especially in the bread aisle, where there was nary a crumb to be had.

"Do you think you'll have any bread tomorrow?" I asked a woman working there.

"No," she confided. "I'm trying to stay away from carbs."

—MARY HANGLEY

DUMB
CUSTOMERS

If there's one lesson from the reams of dumb-customer stories out there, it's this:

WE'RE AT OUR WORST WHEN WE'RE AT OUR NEEDIEST.

When we're hungry, we berate waitresses and hit windows. When our computers confuse us, we shout obscenities at the techies who are our only hope. When we're desperate for that last-minute gift we should have ordered months ago, we hurl insults at hapless retailers.

And when our eruptions are over and we walk out of the store, we blithely forget what we just did, safe in the knowledge that the customer is always right:

Did it rain at the lake? "We want our parking money back!"

Are the tacos too spicy? "We're calling the cops!"

Is the sand on the beach too hot, the hotel bed too comfortable, the buffet loaded with too much food that tastes too good? "We pay your salary you know! We'll be sending nasty letters until we get a #$% refund!"

In many ways it makes perfect sense. Ours is a consumer economy, built on free- market principles, and anyone who can manage to bring a few bucks to a drive-through window can instantly become a Ruler of the Universe. Woe betide the poor wage slave who can't deliver the king's chicken nuggets fast enough.

So the study of the Dumb Customer is, in fact, a kind of look in the mirror. And our reflection isn't always pretty.

Sometimes we're plain crazy, like the man who was asked not to smoke in a bar and responded by firing up a chain saw and attacking the other patrons.

Other times, we're rude, like the nonstop yakkers who led one Los Angeles restaurant to offer discounts to customers who would stay off their cell phones.

But more often than not, we're just oblivious. And while business owners will put up with a lot, there is a limit.

Take, for example, this tale from a market in the shore town of Harvey Cedars, New Jersey. The store had a long practice of "reserving" newspapers for vacationers who wanted to make sure they got their paper, even if they slept late.

It was an old-fashioned courtesy from a small business in a small town—that little extra effort that provides the personal touch we all love.

And it lasted until the day the owner got a note that read:

Al: I would like to reserve a **New York Times, Star-Ledger** *and* **Post** *for every Saturday, Sunday, and Monday from June 22 'til Labor Day. However, we will be in Greece from July 1 to July 8. My son may, or may not, pick up the papers then, we don't know. We will be in Spain for two weeks in August, not sure which two though, we'll try to let you know. Oh, and we don't need the* **Times** *on any Mondays in July, except the 8th of July."*

The shop soon responded with a notice of its own: "Effective July 15, we will no longer be reserving newspapers. We appreciate your understanding."

And truly, who wouldn't understand?

The Customer Is Always Right

Last fall, a vacationer called to make a reservation at my campground. But first, she had a question: "Can you tell me what day the leaves change color?"

—PAMELA BROWN

A scene from our bookshop:

Customer: Hey there, can you help me find a book?

Me: Of course, ma'am. Do you know the author or title?

Customer: Well you see, I was at the beach and I saw this girl reading a purple book. She looked like she was really enjoying it! I want that book.

Me: Ma'am, you're going to have to be more specific. There are a lot of books with purple covers.

Customer: Can't you search on your computer for purple books?

Me: Unfortunately, no.

Customer: I'll go to a bookstore that has better computers.

—STUPIDCOWORKERS.COM

My friend was working at an amusement park when a couple stopped him. "Excuse me," said the woman, pointing to a pond. "What is that water made out of?"

Bemused, my friend replied, "Two parts hydrogen and one part oxygen."

"See?" she said to her boyfriend. "I told you it wasn't real."

—AMELIA WINES

A young blonde, on vacation in Louisiana, wanted a pair of genuine alligator shoes, but was reluctant to pay high New Orleans prices. "I'll just catch my own alligator," she told one shopkeeper, "so I can get a pair of shoes for free." She stomped out of the store and headed for the swamp.

Later, as the shopkeeper drove home, he spotted the blonde standing waist-deep in a bayou, shotgun in hand, with a huge alligator closing in. She took aim and shot the creature between the eyes. The shopkeeper watched in amazement as she struggled to haul the carcass onto an embankment where several other dead alligators were lined up. "Oh, no!" the blonde shouted in dismay. "This one isn't wearing any shoes either!"

—LOUIS B. MCINTOSH

A customer called our service line demanding help with her TV set, which wouldn't come on.

"I'm sorry, but we can't send a technician out today due to the blizzard," I told her.

Unsatisfied, she barked, "I need my TV fixed today! What else am I supposed to do while the power is out?"

—ARIELLE MOBLEY

Low on gas while on a vacation trip to Las Vegas, I pulled my van into a service station. As I was turning in, I spied lying on the ground a gas cap that looked like it might replace my missing one. I hurriedly parked by the pump, jumped out of the van, ran over and picked up the cap. I was pleasantly surprised to find that it screwed easily onto my tank.

A perfect fit, I thought. And then I noticed the keyhole in the top of the cap.

—BOB SJOSTRAND

DUMB CUSTOMERS

A shopper at my in-laws' clothing store couldn't understand why she had to pay so much for her purchase.

"I got this from the '15 to 35% Percent Off' rack," she complained. "And I pick 35 percent."

—KATY GIBBS

I was struggling to separate one shopping cart from another at the supermarket when a fellow customer came to my aid.

"It seems to be shopping cart mating season," I joked.

"I certainly hope so," she said, tugging on one. "They never have enough carts at this store."

—MARJORIE KNOWLES

The Mexican restaurant looked great. Only one problem: it wasn't open. So I jotted down the name for another day.

Just then, a man came out of the restaurant and took a peek at what I'd written. "That's not the name of the restaurant," he said, pointing to the sign over the door. "That's Spanish for, 'Closed on Mondays.'"

—BETTIE WRIGHT

Although I am of Chinese descent, I never really learned to speak Chinese. One evening, I came home boasting about a wonderful meal I'd had in Chinatown. Unfortunately, I couldn't remember the name of the restaurant, but was able to write the Chinese character that was on the door and show it to my mother.

"Do you know what it says?" Mom asked with a smile. "It says 'Pull.'"

—BARBARA MAO

One holiday season, a customer came in with a receipt to ask if we could deliver her layaway purchase by Christmas.

I looked over her paperwork and realized there might be a problem. "We can't guarantee it will arrive before Christmas, because you didn't pay it off by the first of the month," I said.

"What? Are you trying to ruin Christmas?" she cried. "My grandchildren will find out there is no Santa! Nobody told me I had to pay it off by then!"

"I'm sorry, all the terms and conditions were printed on your receipt," I said, pointing to her signature. "See, you signed to say that you accepted them."

The customer stared at the receipt and the rules it spelled out, and then looked back at me. "But nobody TOLD me to read them!"

—STUPIDCOWORKERS.COM

I work in an Italian restaurant. One evening a woman asked, "Is here squid in your calamari?"

What could I say? "Yes," I replied.

That wasn't want my customer wanted to hear. "I only like the rings," she said. "I hate the squid."

—STUCKSERVING.COM

"FDA Approves 3rd Breast Implant"

—ASSOCIATED PRESS

DUMB CUSTOMERS

The waitress was refilling cups of coffee when she stopped at the table next to ours.

"Regular?" she asked the customer.

"Yes, thank you," said the man. "Due to a steady diet of fruit."

—JANET LUNDQUIST

Because our new refrigerator was taller than our old one, I told my wife I'd have to cut away part of an overhanging cabinet to make it fit. Not wanting to mess it up, I called a local radio home-fixit program for advice. I was in the middle of getting the instructions when my wife burst into the room. "You won't believe this," she said, "but there's a guy on the radio with the same problem!"

—GARY BRINGHURST

A customer walked into our electronics store knowing exactly what she wanted: "Can you show me an ovulating fan?" she asked me.

I was tongue-tied, but another clerk wasn't. "You don't want one," he told her. "They only work once a month."

—JAMES RICHARDS

A scene from our ice cream shop:

Customer: I'd like one scoop of strawberry.

Me: Cup or cone?

Customer: Do you have any cones that are edible?

Me: All of our cones are edible.

Customer: Can I take it with me on the beach?

Me: All our cones are entirely portable.

Customer: Do you have any that don't crunch?

—STUPIDCOWORKERS.COM

You Put What Where?

Customer expectations aren't always easy to manage—especially when the customers are expecting to get their money back. Here's a list of the most unlikely insurance claims for lost and damaged cell phones, from mobileinsurance.co.uk:

- *A farmer in Devon lost his phone inside a cow while using its flashlight app during the birth of a calf. The phone later reappeared but was, um, damaged.*

- *A Nottingham woman accidentally baked her Nokia 6303i into her daughter's birthday cake.*

- *A woman in Wales was walking her dog on the beach when, she claimed, a seagull plucked her Samsung Galaxy from her hand. Another customer reported that monkeys had stolen his HTC One X while he filmed them in a safari park.*

- *A Bristol woman reported that her BlackBerry's "vibrate" function broke while she was using it as an adult toy.*

- *A couple on a cruise dropped their phone overboard while they tried to photograph themselves striking the famous* I'm the King of the World! *pose from the movie* Titanic.

- *A pyrotechnician setting up a fireworks show in Plymouth left his iPhone 3GS in the "blast zone," where it was shot three thousand feet in the air. No report on where it came down.*

- *A Liverpool woman broke her HTC Desire X when she threw it at her cheating boyfriend and hit a wall instead.*

We love our fast food—but some of us love it too much. Here's a sample of the kind of "restaurant rage" afflicting unhappy customers all over the world:

● *A Toledo woman wanted an order of McNuggets at 6 a.m.— but the drive-through attendant told her it was too early. So first the woman tried to punch the attendant. Then she punched another employee. Then she threw a bottle through the drive-through window. She didn't get her McNuggets, but she did get 60 days in prison.*

—SOURCE: NEW YORK DAILY NEWS

● *A Georgia man was unhappy with the chalupas he'd brought home from his Taco Bell—he felt there wasn't enough meat inside, and he called the restaurant to complain. The manager told him she couldn't do anything that night as the restaurant was closing. "That's all right, I'll come by and redecorate the place," he said. He soon returned with a Molotov cocktail to try to burn the restaurant down. He failed—but he never got caught, either.*

—SOURCE: THESMOKINGGUN.COM

● *An angry customer called the police to McDonald's in Guangzhou, China, because he believed the Spicy McChicken he'd been given was too spicy. He got a free meal out of it.*

—SOURCE: KOTAKU.COM

● *An Englishwoman tried to ride her horse through her local McDonald's drive-through, but was told that she'd have to come inside for service. Naturally she brought the horse inside, where it promptly did what horses do. "The horse*

ended up doing his business on the floor," reported the
Greater Manchester Police, who gave her a ticket for "causing
alarm and distress" to customers and staff.

—SOURCE: NEWSFEED.TIME.COM

A guy walks into a hardware store and says, "I want a chain saw
that will cut down ten trees in an hour." So the clerk sells him one.

The next day, the customer comes in, upset. "This chain saw cut
down only one little tree in an hour!"

The clerk says, "Let me take a look."

He pulls the starter rope, the saw roars to life, and the customer
screams, "What's that noise!?"

—CHERYL WITTLE

I was working as a flight attendant on a flight to Milan when
a passenger beckoned me down the aisle. He complained of a
headache and asked, "What's that dull whirring sound?"

"It's the engines, sir," I replied.

You'd think that would have ended it—but you'd be wrong.
The passenger demanded I tell the captain to turn the engines
off, as his head was really sore. Furthermore, he said, he'd be
complaining further to the airline, because the terms and conditions
on his ticket "did not state how loud the engines were during
the flight."

—CABINCREW.COM

A customer who bought a book from me through Amazon.com
left a poor rating. The reason: "The book was dated." The title of the
book was *Victorian Fancy Stitchery*.

—MOIRA ALLEN

A customer called me in a lather about his credit card bill: "I keep seeing a charge for $9.99 on my account," he said. "Why do you people keep charging me $9.99?"

"Sir, that charge is coming not from us, but from GGW," I replied.

"What the @#$% is GGW?" he shot back. "People are stealing my money and you do nothing! So what the #$% is GGW?"

This was no mystery to me. We see that charge all the time. "Sir," I said, "GGW stands for Girls Gone—"

I didn't have to finish. "Oh yeah," he said. "Never mind. I remember now . . . uh . . . bye."

—STUPIDCOWORKERS.COM

I was working at a bar and grill that featured outdoor seating. One evening a customer walked in, and I asked her if she would like to sit inside or out on the patio.

The customer—who'd walked through the parking lot just moments before—replied, "I don't know, is it cold out there?"

—STUCKSERVING.COM

"Hooker Named Lay Person of the Year"

—*DEKALB NEWS*

Not the Sharpest Tool in the Shed

Larry wins the lottery and dashes downtown to claim his prize. "Give me my $20 million," he tells the man in charge.

"Sorry, but it doesn't work that way," the man says. "You'll get a million today, and then the rest will be spread out over the next 19 years."

Larry is furious. "Look, I want my money! And if you're not going to give me my $20 million right now, then I want my dollar back!"

—MIKE BROWNING

Jim arrives home to find his wife lying on the floor in a pool of sweat. He rushes over and rouses her. It's then that he notices that she's wearing a parka and a mink.

"Are you okay? What are you doing?" he asks.

"You've been promising to paint the living room for months now," she explains groggily. "I wanted to prove that I could do just as good a job as you, and faster too."

"Well, it does look like you did a good job," Jim says, looking around. "But why are you all bundled up?"

"I know how to read," she snaps. "The can said, 'For best results put on two coats.'"

—CORA M. BOGGS

After hearing stories about radioactivity in granite countertops, my wife became alarmed.

"I have granite in my kitchen," she told a friend.

"Maybe you should get a Geiger counter," her friend suggested.

My wife was intrigued. "Are those the granite imitations they sell at Costco?"

—DANIEL OSTER

A customer walked into our autoparts store looking for a flat washer. "That'll be 15 cents," I said.

"Fifteen cents for a washer? Are you crazy?" he yelled. "I'll drill a hole in a quarter and make my own."

—JACK REEVES

My niece was thrilled to hear that a new car wash was opening up in her neighborhood.

"How convenient," she said. "I can walk to it."

—CATHY MCCOURT

I answer a lot of questions at the information desk at Olympic National Park, in Washington State. But one visitor stumped me: "Do you have any trails that just go downhill?"

—MIKE PERZEL

One day at our hotel, we got a string of calls from a man claiming to be a guest's boss. He told us that our guest wasn't returning his message and asked us to track her down.

I called the guest and said, "Hello! I received a few phone calls from a Mr. Jones [not his real name] asking you to call him back immediately."

"Mr. Jones? I don't know a Mr. Jones," she answered.

"Okay. I'm sorry to bother you," I said. "I'll ask him to stop calling."

"Well, what was his name again?" she asked.

"Mr. Jones," I said.

"Was he tall?" she asked.

That stumped me. "Ma'am, he was on the phone."

"You didn't notice if he was tall or not? That doesn't help me at all."

Rule No. 1: when in doubt, be polite. "Very sorry, ma'am," I said. "I will try to get a better look at him next time he calls."

"Thank you so much, dear!" she replied and hung up.

—STUPIDCOWORKERS.COM

A customer called our florist shop to order a bouquet. "Make it bright and festive looking," she said. "I want it to cheer up a friend. She just lost her Seeing Eye dog."

—HARRY CHALKLY

Customer: Your escalators are broken.

Security: What do you mean by broken?

Customer: They aren't moving.

Security: Okay. Which one is it?

The customer leads the security guard to the "escalator" and stands on the top step: See? Broken.

Security: Sir, those are stairs.

—STUPIDCOWORKERS.COM

A customer came into our store with a printed set of directions and a problem:

"Pardon me, sir. I'm lost. Can you help me, please?"

"Sure," I said. "What are you looking for?"

"I'm looking for Milkjer Boulevard." he said.

That wasn't familiar at all. "I've never heard of it," I answered.

"Yeah, it's a weird spelling," he said. "But it's clearly Milkjer Boulevard."

"Can I see your directions?" I asked.

"Sure," the customer said. "See, it's spelled M-L-K-J-r Blvd."

—STUPIDCOWORKERS.COM

A customer at our bookstore asked me, "Do you have the original book Romeo and Juliet? My daughter needs it for school, and all I can find is the play."

—AUDRIE WESTON

DUMB CUSTOMERS

Nobody Complains Like the Brits

Maybe it's the fact that they live on a damp, gray island, but even on holiday, the English can bring the customer complaints like nobody else on earth. The travel agency Sunshine.co.uk compiled its favorites:

- *A visitor to the sunny Canary Islands complained the sand was too hot for her children's feet.*

- *A guest at a Costa del Sol resort complained that there was too much food at the buffet and that he'd put on "at least" five pounds as a result.*

- *A gentleman visiting Majorca complained that he'd had a falling out with his wife because the beaches were too full of beautiful women in bikinis, at whom he'd been caught gaping "on more than one occasion."*

- *An English couple hoping for something "exotic" said their two weeks in Turkey were spoiled because there were "too many English people around."*

- *A visitor to Portugal complained that his hotel bed was "too comfy," leading him to oversleep when he would have "preferred to be up early and making the most of it."*

- *A traveler to Bulgaria complained about the loud lovemaking of the couple next door. The problem being that it made him feel "pressured" into making love to his own wife.*

A friend and I decided to check out a little boutique in the country. While we were examining the china, curios, and hand-crocheted tablecloths, a man appeared.

"Can I help you?" he asked.

"No, thank you," I said. "We're just browsing in your lovely boutique."

He politely responded, "The boutique is downstairs; this is our living room."

—PATRICIA REGAN

Overheard in a hotel lobby in Bora-Bora:

Vacationer: We have lizards in our bungalow, and my wife is freaking out. I didn't pay to have lizards in my room!

Desk clerk: No problem, sir. We will be sure to add that to your bill.

—BILLY DOBRUCKY

I work the switchboard at a large insurance company. With thousands of employees, I need a first and last name to make the right connection, so when a customer called asking to be "transferred to Mike," I said, "Sure, what's Mike's last name?"

"I'm not sure, I just know his first name is Mike," the caller answered.

"I'm sorry, but we have hundreds of Mikes, so I would need a last name," I said.

"Oh, I see," said the caller. "Well, I'll just call him and get his last name, then."

"Okay," I replied. "But if you have his direct number, why were you calling me in the first place?"

I never learned the answer; the customer hung up.

—STUPIDCOWORKERS.COM

DUMB
911

If there's any reason to pay attention to dumb criminals, it's this:

THEY'LL TEACH YOU HOW NOT TO GET CAUGHT.

For example:

> *If you plan to use a fake name, don't tattoo your real name on your head.*
>
> *If you want to rob a store, don't leave behind your address, or a T-shirt with your face on it.*
>
> *If you want money for nothing, don't try to counterfeit a million dollar bill or cash a billion dollar check.*
>
> *And if you want to steal change from somebody's glove compartment, don't leave your cell phone behind with your mom's number prominently listed.*

You'd think those sorts of things would be self-evident, but to the good citizens you'll meet in this chapter, they weren't. That's the hallmark of dumb criminals everywhere: they fail because they overlook the blindingly obvious.

Excited by the prospect of easy money, sex, and drugs, they hatch elaborate, daring plans but forget to work through all the details. They wake up in bed thinking, "Today's the big day—nothing can go wrong!" And they fall asleep behind bars thinking, "How could I have been so stupid?"

Like the guy who robbed a bank in Syracuse; he didn't get all the cash he wanted, so he went back for more and got arrested.

Like the guy in New York who used his brother's name as an alias but forgot that his brother was a wanted man too.

Like the guy on parole in Ohio who allegedly decided to rob a string of homes but forgot that the GPS unit on his ankle bracelet allowed the police to track his every move.

Crooks don't just want money or drugs; they want notoriety and bragging rights. Take, for example, the three guys who liked their Del Taco free-taco scam so much that they put it on YouTube—where everyone saw it, including the cops who eventually arrested them.

And lawbreakers aren't the only folks we'll learn from in this chapter. The foolishness fielded by 911 operators teaches us that our nation is full of people who aren't exactly thinking clearly. They call because their hamburgers taste funny; they call because their wives have their beer; they call because their phones aren't working. One man was arrested for making 27,000 calls for no other reason than "because they were free."

So the lessons dumb criminals teach us are clear: plan well, keep your mouth shut, and don't let greed or pride blind you to important details that can jump up and bite you in the butt.

After all, whether you're a criminal or a cop, if you let your ego get ahead of your planning, your Big Moment can turn into Big Stupid real fast. Take the story from Snopes.com of the DEA agent who showed off his Glock pistol during a safety class in Florida. "I am the only one professional enough in the room to carry one," he said proudly—just before shooting himself in the leg.

Help! Send Police! I'm Dumb!

When Jonathan Huntley was released from prison after seven years, the 25-year-old North Carolina man celebrated by making a T-shirt featuring his mug shot and the slogan, "Making Money Is My Thang."

He was charged with breaking into a house, where he allegedly stole a bunch of cash and jewelry, and somehow left behind his shirt. It didn't take the cops long to track him down, but the charges were quickly dismissed.

—THESMOKINGGUN.COM

After stealing surveillance cameras from a Garden Grove, California, business, Howard Shanholtzer ditched the white Mitsubishi pickup truck cops knew he drove and stole another vehicle.

"Unfortunately for him," said Detective Paul Danielson, "the car he stole was also a white Mitsubishi pickup truck." Shanholtzer was quickly arrested.

—READER'S DIGEST

The 911 system has long been America's lifeline—our instant connection to the forces of justice. But like anything available to everyone, it's subject to, shall we say, questionable uses, and 911 abuse is now a crime. Here's a selection from The Smoking Gun website, of callers who started out looking for help and ended up getting busted:

● *Donna Marie Nichols called 911 after biting into a Hardee's hamburger that proved unsatisfactory. She called the restaurant to complain, and was offered a cash refund, but she refused. Then she called the police. "I only took a small*

bite and it's nasty," she told the operator. She probably didn't
find the food in jail much better.

- Michael Alan Skopec called 911 to complain about his phone.
  "Why is my iPhone not working? Why can't I dial the numbers
  I used to be able to dial?" he asked the operator. "My
  emergency is my @#$% phone don't work." After he called
  five times, police went to his home to investigate him and
  found—astonishingly—that he'd been drinking.

- John Bansley called 911 when his ex-wife wouldn't release his
  prized possession: five cans of cold Milwaukee's Best beer.
  He'd been dropped by police at her house after being picked
  up for drinking in public, and she apparently didn't want
  him to continue drinking in private. After convincing the 911
  operator to send an officer, Bansley asked the operator, "You
  got a personal phone number? You sound kinda pretty." She
  laughed—and he got arrested.

- Never accuse 86-year-old, 98-pound Dorothy Densmore of
  giving in to old age. She wanted a slice of pizza delivered to
  her home, but when her local pizza place told her they'd only
  deliver a whole pie, she made more than twenty 911 calls to
  complain. An officer soon visited her home, and in addition to
  being charged with misusing the system, she was charged
  with resisting arrest for allegedly kicking, scratching, and
  biting him.

Phillip Williams, a security guard at an air force base, was an
unhappy consumer. So he stopped two Tampa, Florida, police
officers, handed over his crack pipe, and asked if they wouldn't
mind testing the crack cocaine that he'd bought earlier, just to
make sure it was the real deal. Good news! It was. Bad news! They
arrested him.

—REALPOLICE.NET

DUMB 911

Big Plans, Poor Planning

It sure didn't take a master sleuth to catch these bumbling crooks. Who knew that shop-lifting could be a perfect Kodak moment? A thief and his sidekick seemed pretty savvy when they entered a Long Island Wal-Mart and swept the shelves of $2,000 worth of digital cameras. A store worker found only an abandoned shopping cart filled with empty camera boxes.

Meanwhile, the store's surveillance tape looked like it was going to be useless: The video showed the suspects, a man and a woman, but the images were far too grainy to identify them. Then security officials noticed that, at one point, the tape showed the woman picked up a demonstration camera that was chained to a counter, and pointed it at her partner. No, she couldn't have . . . Yes, she did. The store's manager called over to the Wal-Mart photo center and asked about the camera. All they had to do was press the print button to see exactly what the picture on the disc looked like. Out popped a clear color image of a balding man with a mustache, looking straight at the camera. The police couldn't ask for a better mug shot. Shortly after the robbery, Suffolk Police Detective Sgt. Paul Dodorico said he thought the couple "will be kind of surprised. I'm sure they thought there was nothing in the camera."

—READER'S DIGEST

A PNC Bank in Harrisburg, Pennsylvania, was allegedly robbed twice by the same man. The suspect was nabbed when he returned a third time to check his account balance.

—SOURCE: *MECHANICSBURG PATRIOT-NEWS*

During a stickup, a bank robber in Phoenix, Arizona, told the teller to hand over "all the twenties, forties, and sixties."

—SOURCE: *PHOENIX TIMES-HERALD*

Two counterfeiters were arrested in Maryland with fake $100 bills. The clue that gave them away: printed on the front, just to the left of Ben Franklin's face, were the words "Billete de la Suerte Alasitas."

Most likely they were "lucky money" novelty bills from South America's famous Alasitas Festival, held each year in La Paz, Bolivia.

—VOICES.WASHINGTONPOST.COM

An Aiken, South Carolina, man robbed a clerk at a convenience store, then jumped into his getaway vehicle and took off. Police had little trouble catching up with him a short distance away. He was driving a Craftsman riding lawn mower.

—SOURCE: *AIKEN STANDARD*

"Suspect Held in Killing of Reporter for Variety"

—*THE NEW YORK TIMES*

A Connecticut bank received a strange phone call. It was from a pair of would-be robbers requesting that the bank prepare a bag of money for them to pick up a few minutes later. When they arrived, the men found the police waiting instead.

—SOURCE: *ASSOCIATED PRESS*

Consumers in northern Alabama became suspicious when they received recorded messages urging them call a phone number where they could "update" their bank account records. Their caller IDs read: "This is a scam."

—SOURCE: ENEWSCOURIER.COM

Smuggling Dumb

Drugs will make you nuts. For proof, simply observe what people will do to get them over borders and into prisons. Smugglers have been known to stuff drugs into melons, disguise them as powdered soup, sneak them underwater in home-made submarines, and even pack them into corpses. And while plenty succeed, many others get tripped up along the way.

- *A border gang was seen in Mexico using a nine-foot-tall homemade catapult to hurl four-pound bricks of marijuana over the fence into Arizona. "While it doubtless runs afoul of U.S. drug laws," one report noted, "from a diplomatic standpoint, is this considered an act of war or a foreign-aid package?"*

  —SOURCE: POPSCI.COM

- *In 2010, residents near Greenville, Texas, were surprised to find duffel bags of high-grade marijuana falling from the sky. An abandoned plane found nearby suggests that someone's delivery service didn't work out quite as planned.*

  —SOURCE: TRUTV.COM

- *At one US/Mexican border crossing, police dogs went red alert when they sniffed an elderly Mexican woman's seven-pound statue of Jesus. No drugs were found inside the statue, and agents eventually discovered that the entire thing was made of a mix of plaster and cocaine. As Cracked.com put it: "We don't know how exactly they intended to get the drugs back out of the statue. All we know is if one day you find yourself grinding up the head of Jesus so you can snort it, it's probably time to reevaluate your life."*

Police Blotter

Police in Pico Rivera, California, had an easy time pinning a four-year-old murder on 25-year-old Anthony Garcia; he pinned it on himself with an elaborate tattoo on his chest depicting the killing.

Cops noticed the incriminating ink when taking Garcia's mug shot for a petty crime. On close inspection, the tattoo revealed all the details of the night, from the Christmas lights and bent street lamp near the liquor store where the body was found to the image of an angry helicopter—Garcia's nickname was "Chopper"—machine-gunning the victim. Garcia, it turned out, had spent years adding details to the scene, until he was finally ready for his close-up.

—SOURCE: BREAKINGBROWN.COM

Fort Worth, Texas, police arrested Charles Ray Fuller for trying to cash a check made out for $360 billion. Fuller claimed his girlfriend's mother gave him the money to start a record business. The woman denied being that dumb.

—SOURCE: CBSNEWS.COM

Two men were arrested for shoplifting at a back-to-school event at a department store. Their careful planning was thwarted by one small detail: it was the annual "Shop with a Cop" day, when dozens of police officers show up to help children pick out school supplies.

—SOURCE: OREGONLIVE.COM

A 21-year-old man called the police after suspecting he'd just been ripped off. The marijuana he had purchased from a street dealer, he told cops, tasted "nasty," and he wanted them to confirm that the weed was real. Luckily for him, it wasn't.

—SOURCE: PITTSBURGH POST-GAZETTE

"Mother Arrested after Drowning"

—*HOUSTON CHRONICLE*

After a man kicked in the front door of a Texas home at 3:30 a.m., the resident fled and called police. When cops arrived, they were surprised to find that the intruder hadn't stolen a thing. Even more surprising: they found him in the bathroom, enjoying a warm bath.

—SOURCE: *ASSOCIATED PRESS*

Tonya Ann Fowler was furious that an unflattering mug shot taken by police was used to depict her in the local paper, so she called 911 to complain. She was promptly arrested. The good news: police took a new mug shot.

—SOURCE: BLOGS.AJC.COM

Jan Englishman, enraged for some reason by the fact that teenage girls were walking past his house, decided that the thing to do was get his gun and point it at them. When police confronted him, he told them that he forgot he was holding a gun.

—SOURCE: CRACKED.COM

The owner of a Mount Kisco, New York, computer shop convinced a customer that his computer was infected with a virus planted by evil Polish priests linked to the religious organization Opus Dei. The owner convinced the customer to pay for protection and was eventually charged with grand larceny—but not before spending six years billing the terrified customer's credit card for a total of more than $6 million.

—SOURCE: GOTHAMIST.COM

Ohn Browning of the *Rockwall* (Texas) *Herald Banner* passes along this gem from a criminal trial:

Lawyer: Trooper, when you stopped the defendant, were your red and blue lights flashing?

Witness: Yes.

Lawyer: Did the defendant say anything when she got out of her car?

Witness: Yes, sir.

Lawyer: What did she say?

Witness: She said "What disco am I at?"

—ROCKWALLHERALDBANNER.COM

As a burglar tried to enter the home of a Georgia woman, she took matters into her own hands. Getting down on all fours, she barked and scratched feverishly at the door. The thief was last seen running from the porch.

—SOURCE: *ATHENS BANNER HERALD*

Nineteen-year-old Justin MacGilfrey allegedly entered a Daytona Beach, Florida, store, pointed his index finger—yes, his index finger!—at the clerk, cocked his thumb, and demanded all the money in the register. Shocking news: he didn't get it. He did get arrested, though.

—SOURCE: DAILYREVELRY.COM

While searching for murder suspect Sterling F. Wolfname, cops in Billings, Montana, ran into someone at a shelter who matched his description. When they asked him if he was Wolfname, the man said he wasn't. The officers concluded he was fibbing when they spotted this tattoo on his head: Wolfname.

—*READER'S DIGEST*

Excuses, Excuses

Who has a better chance of sounding dumb than a criminal who's just been caught in the act?

- *A homeless man in Santa Cruz, CA was found drunk in the street with a keg of beer, a bag of magic mushrooms, and a wet suit. He told police that he was an Australian secret agent on a covert undercover mission. They didn't believe him.*

- *A South Carolina woman was spotted weaving down Main Street on a stolen horse, slurring her words and reeking of alcohol. When questioned by police, she told them the horse was drunk, not her.*

—SOURCE:CRACKED.COM

- *A Minnesota couple was caught red-handed one evening trying to empty out a woman's house. Police arrived to find their bikes packed with the woman's computers, tools, bicycles, and personal effects. The couple claimed a Craigslist ad listed the place as a "free house" whose owners were moving out and giving everything away. Shockingly, no one else saw the ad, and no record of it was ever found.*

—SOURCE:CRACKED.COM

- *A Swedish woman was pulled over for drunk driving after being spotted swerving across multiple lanes. She was ten times over the legal limit and admitted to seeing double, but told police that she'd compensated by keeping one eye closed.*

—SOURCE: THELOCAL.SE

Some Crooks Aren't So Dumb

You've heard the expression about how "anything that's not nailed down" might get stolen—turns out, some things aren't safe even when they ARE nailed down, or bolted down, or rooted in the earth. Oddee.com rounded up some of the weirdest thefts ever, most of which remain unsolved:

- In 2008, hundreds of tons of sand were stolen from a beach in Coral Spring, Jamaica. Some say the island's resorts support a lively black market in top-quality sand, but "forensic tests" so far haven't revealed where the sand went—much less who took it.

- A group of thieves in the Czech Republic stole a ten-ton railroad bridge and 650 feet of track by pretending to be a demolition crew. They arrived at the depot in Slavkov, flashed some forged documents, and explained that they were clearing things out to make way for a new bike path. "It was only after they had gone that we realized we'd been had," a railroad spokesperson said.

- A West African born street entertainer's record-breaking egg hat—a towering bonnet featuring 642 hard-boiled eggs— was stolen from a hospital in Germany while he recovered from a case of heatstroke (brought on, quite possibly, by the effort of performing in the summer sun while carrying 50 pounds of eggs on his head). "It is my whole way of life," explained Greg da Silva, a former computer scientist now known as the Famous Eggman, "but I know Germans are very honest people and I am sure someone will hand it in."

Small Town Trouble

Even the police had to smile at this one. It was a case of passing counterfeit money that brought cops in Roanoke Rapids, North Carolina, to a local supermarket. There they got a look at the bogus bill. Was it a bad likeness of Jefferson on the $20, or maybe of Grant on the $50? Nope. It was a fairly sharp Presidential likeness, actually—of George W. Bush on a $200 bill.

On the back of the note, police found an image of the White House, with its South Lawn cluttered with signs reading "We like broccoli" and "USA deserves a tax cut." Pretty goofy to think you could get away with that as payment for groceries, right? Well, this is a case of dumb and dumber. The supermarket cashier actually accepted the phony bill, and gave the customer his groceries along with $50 in change. Apprehended 12 days later, the man with the funny money was ordered to pay back the store—in real bills, thank you—and then released.

—READER'S DIGEST

Police are by no means immune to the power of dumb, and as everyone knows, nothing melts the brain faster than the sight of a pile of hard currency.

That may be what happened to the cops in Moorhead, Minnesota, who received a very unusual visit from a waitress. Stacy Knudson was working at the Fryn' Pan Restaurant when a customer left her a $12,000 tip in a cardboard box. Being a God-fearing, law-abiding Minnesotan, and worried that the money might be stolen, Knudson took the money to the police and turned it in.

At the time, the cops told her she could have it if no one claimed it. So far, so good. But when three months had passed and Knudson returned, the police changed their tune: because the money smelled of marijuana, they said, they would have to keep it.

Knudson was offered a $1,000 reward in exchange, but, being a God-fearing, law-abiding Minnesotan who felt like she was getting ripped off, she filed suit instead. The story quickly went national—and the Moorhead police quickly turned over the cash.

—MENTALFLOSS.COM

In case you doubted that our nation is a seething hotbed of dangerous criminal activity, consider these reports of chaos and mayhem, culled from the blog Extremely Trivial Police Reports:

● *"Call of a dead possum on Pleasant Street. Caller states that he will put it in a bag."*

● *"Caller on Sagamore Avenue came to the station to report that his roommate may have stolen his laptop and could possibly be a Russian spy."*

● *"A man arrived with a stab wound to his upper thigh. He said he had opened the knife to protect himself at a party then put it back in his pocket . . . forgetting to close the knife. A strange story but lacerated pants and flesh were consistent with statements. We took the knife for safekeeping."*

You Have the Right to Remain Silent

A 17-year-old suspected arsonist approached a car in Lambertville, Michigan, intending to siphon gas from it. What he forgot to do was ask permission from the detective sitting in the front seat.

—READER'S DIGEST

Alexander D. Smith walked into an Augusta, Georgia, bank and tried to open an account with a $1 million bill. Great idea—except there is no such thing as a $1 million bill.

—READER'S DIGEST

Robert Echeverria, 32, scammed a Rialto, California, Del Taco by calling up and pretending he was a local CEO whose order had been botched.

Echeverria was so pleased with the $15 in free eats, he and two friends shot a short movie called *How to Scam Del Taco* and posted it on YouTube. It proved popular, especially among cops, who watched it and promptly arrested the would-be executive.

—PYSIH.COM

Scottish shoplifter Aron Morrison was picked up after pinching a bottle of vodka from a liquor store. It didn't take Sherlock Holmes to find Morrison, especially since he'd left his name and phone number with the clerk after asking her out on a date.

—RD.COM

Receiving a report of a man banging on a door at 3:30 in the morning, police responded to a mini-mart in Ossining, New York. When officers arrived, they chased Blake Leak, 23, through the streets and down an embankment. It looked bleak for Leak, until both cops took a tumble. Seizing the opportunity, he sought refuge on the grounds of a large building. Unfortunately, it turned out to be a well-known local landmark, the Sing Sing maximum security prison, where he was nabbed by a guard.

—LOHUD.COM

"Homocide Victims Rarely Talk to Police"

—THE EXPRESS-TIMES

Convicted of receiving stolen property, James Wombles, 37, had to wear an ankle bracelet as a part of his parole. The bracelet came complete with a GPS monitoring system that let cops track his every move.

Over the course of a few weeks, the Riverside, Ohio, man allegedly broke into six homes. You know where this is going—just as the cops knew where Wombles was going. Following the signals from his bracelet, they tracked him to his car, where they found him sitting on the stolen booty.

—READER'S DIGEST

DUMB
GOES TO
COURT

AH, THE LAW.

Protector of liberty, majestic in its beauty, the law is the glue that binds society and elevates us above the rude beasts.

"At his best, man is the noblest of all animals," the great Greek philosopher Aristotle once said, "separated from law and justice, he is the worst."

And then there is . . . the law. Refuge of the scoundrel, tool of the fool, the law is a whirlpool of choking red tape and point-parsing hairsplittery that can capture even the proudest enterprise, suck it under the waves, and drown it like a cat in a sack.

"The law," wrote Charles Dickens, "is a ass—a idiot."

Yep, that's the law. Is there any institution more widely reviled? Today, approximately 22 percent of the Internet is made up of lawyer jokes. What do you call five thousand lawyers at the bottom of the sea? *A good start.* What do lawyers use as birth control? *Their personalities.*

Yes, everyone agrees, lawyers are the scum of the earth, and judges and other court officials aren't far behind.

And yet, when we find ourselves in trouble, who do we call? *A lawyer.*

> *There's the guy in New York City who got drunk, fell onto the subway tracks, and lost a leg. He called a lawyer, and won a $2.3 million settlement.*

> *There's the woman from Vancouver, Washington, who suffered complications from liposuction performed by a shady doctor she found in the*

phone book. She called a lawyer, sued the phone-book company, and won $1.2 million.

Stories like these are legend in American jurisprudence, and the supply is apparently bottomless. What they tell us is that the same law that makes our society possible and protects us from injustice and abuse of all kinds also provides us with the greatest collection of half-witted nonsense ever assembled.

After all, there is no issue so dumb that some lawyer, somewhere is not prepared to sue over it.

Take Dale Cox, an attorney who once complained to the Cleveland Browns football team about fans throwing paper airplanes in the stands. "As you know, there is the risk of serious eye injury and perhaps an ear injury," Cox wrote. "I will hold you responsible for any injury sustained by any person in my party attending one of your sporting events."

The Browns' lawyer, to his everlasting credit, responded appropriately. "Dear Mr. Cox," he wrote, "I feel that you should be aware that some asshole is signing your name to stupid letters."

So yes, the world is full of dumb lawyers and dumb lawsuits. But the fact is, the world is also full of other kinds of dummies against whom the law is our only protection.

When some TGI Fridays restaurants were replacing top-shelf liquor with cheap swill, the law stepped in. When the mayor of New York City tried to ban large sodas, the law stepped in.

Our world may be full to the brim with bizarre legal news, inane lawsuits and laughable courtroom exchanges like the ones you'll read here. So look, dear reader, and laugh—but don't forget that when some overzealous mayor comes for your soda, it won't be a bottled-water salesman that gets your call.

It'll be your lawyer.

1001 Questions

Lawyer: Did you see the defendant bite off the victim's nose?

Witness: No.

Lawyer: Then how do you know he bit off the victim's nose?

Witness: I saw him spit it out.

—MARY LOUISE GILMAN, *HUMOR IN THE COURT*

Lawyer: You seem to have more than the average share of intelligence for a man of your background.

Witness: If I wasn't under oath, I'd return the compliment.

—MARY LOUISE GILMAN, *HUMOR IN THE COURT*

"**D**oes anyone in this room need to be dismissed from jury duty?" my father, a judge, asked a roomful of prospective jurors.

A nervous young man stood up. "I'd like to be dismissed," he said.

"And why is that?"

"My wife is about to conceive."

Slightly taken aback, Dad responded, "I believe, sir, you mean 'deliver.' But either way, I agree. You should be there."

—BETH DUNCAN

A man is on trial for armed robbery. The jury comes back with the verdict. The foreman stands, clears his throat, and announces, "Not guilty."

The defendant leaps to his feet. "Awesome!" he shouts. "Does that mean I get to keep the money?"

—LAWRENCE ADELSON

An attorney I worked with at a personal-injury law firm deeply resented the term ambulance chaser.

"It's not right to call us that," he told me. "Besides, we usually get there before the ambulances do."

—BRIAN MAYER

While prosecuting a robbery case, I conducted an interview with the arresting officer. My first question: Did you see the defendant at the scene?"

"Yes, from a block away," the officer answered.

"Was the area well lit?"

"No. It was pretty dark."

"Then how could you identify the defendant?" I asked, concerned.

Looking at me as if I were nuts, he answered, "I'd recognize my cousin anywhere."

—MORRISON LEWIS, JR.

I was the court stenographer the day a teenager, who'd been in drug rehab, came before the judge. He told the court how he was gradually overcoming his addiction. The judge was impressed. "Well done," he said. "Let's hope you end the year on a high."

—PHILIP HORTON

JUST DESSERTS

Prison, it turns out, is a great place to learn about tort law. Three inmates from the Kane County Jail in Illinois sued the county sheriff and Aramark food services in 2007 for supplying prisoners with subpar food, including soggy cookies and cakes. The $2 million they sought would buy them a nice drying rack for their desserts.

No luck for these prisoners—the judge dismissed the case.

—READER'S DIGEST

Warning!

Product warnings can't stop every accident. As one wag put it, "You can make it foolproof, but you can't make it damn-fool proof."

But rest assured, if there's a label on a product telling you not to do something, that means somebody else did it already—and sued over it.

And if the product warning labels lawyers now demand are any indication, Americans are shorter on common sense than ever. *Woman's Day* magazine rounded up some of the dumbest:

- *Duraflame Fire Logs: "Warning: Risk of fire."*

- *Terrestrial Digital Outdoor Antenna: "Do not attempt to install if drunk, pregnant, or both."*

- *Rowenta Iron: "Do not aim steam at people or animals, or iron clothes while they are being worn."*

- *Child's Superman costume: "Wearing of this product does not enable you to fly."*

- *Dremel Electric Drill: "Rotary tool. This product is not intended for use as a dental drill."*

- *Razor Go-Kart: "This product moves when used."*

- *Black Cat Fireworks: "Do not put in mouth."*

- *iPod shuffle: "Do not eat."*

- *Kraft Cheese: "For best results, remove cap."*

Charlotte Feeney says blondes have more fun, and that's why she sued cosmetics giant L'Oréal for $15,000. Feeney insisted her life was ruined when she accidentally touched up her naturally flaxen locks with brown dye from a mislabeled box.

"I was sick to my stomach," she said in an affidavit. "I have a bad hair day every day. I had headaches. I don't like myself. I stay home more than ever in my life. I wear hats most of the time." What's more, she told her doctor that she doesn't know how to dress now that she's no longer a blonde—one reason her doctor prescribed medication to treat anxiety and depression.

So why didn't she dye her hair blonde and wait for her natural color to grow back? Who knows, but the real question is, What's wrong with being a raven-haired beauty? "Blondes get more attention than brunettes," she said. "Emotionally, I miss that."

The judge dismissed the suit, ruling that Feeney never proved that L'Oréal was to blame *for the mix-up.*

—*READER'S DIGEST*

"Federal Agents Raid Gun Shop, Find Weapons"

—*TULSA WORLD*

"Your honor," began the defense attorney, "my client has been characterized as an incorrigible bank robber, without a single socially redeeming feature. I intend to disprove that."

"And how will you accomplish this?" the judge inquired.

"By proving beyond a shadow of a doubt," replied the lawyer, "that the note my client handed the teller was on recycled paper."

—R.C. SHEBELSKI

Some parents are ready for anything—including a lawsuit from other parents. That's what one family found out when their daughter was invited to the neighbors' house to play. As reported on the blog Free-Range Kids:

> *Yesterday my daughter came home from playing at the "new" neighbor's house with a four-page liability waiver that they want us to sign! Wow! I guess that dangers lurk over there—in the form of a trampoline—and if she is going to set foot on their property, she needs a release first. I can't help but feel paranoid—should I then be worried about having their kids over at our house, because the first thing in their mind is legal action? Has anyone heard of such a thing? Is this the new normal for making friends?*

Luckily, it's still not normal—but it's not unprecedented. In 1999, according to Overlawyered.com, one New York family decided that their daughter's sleepover party could not proceed unless all the invitees signed a release waiving "all present and future claims related to or arising out of or in connection with the visit or any losses they, any other family member or any third party may suffer in connection therewith . . . "

The other families from the young lady's expensive private school apparently understood the need for such legalities and signed the waivers.

But if such legal madness remains rare, legal expert Jonathan Turley still saw an opportunity to make a few bucks and laughs. "I would encourage any parents wanting a liability-safe playdate to contact me for waiver drafting," Turley wrote, with tongue firmly planted in cheek. "I may need suggestions on the slogan." Some examples:

● *BECAUSE NO CHILD SHOULD BE WITHOUT HIS LAWYER*

● *GIVE YOUR CHILD THE GIFT OF REPRESENTATION*

- *LIKE A SECOND [CONTINGENCY-BASED] FATHER*

- *IF YOU HAVE A WEDGIE, YOU HAVE A LAWYER*

- *BECAUSE SUE IS NOT JUST A CUTE NAME*

Nobody knows the pain of ugly courtroom battles better than the judges who must preside over them. And those judges love nothing more than seeing all parties settle up and get the heck out.

But few judges are as visibly delighted by such settlements as shown in Consumerist.com in the piece by Judge Martin J. Sheehan of Kentucky, who was so happy to see a legal malpractice suit wrap up that he penned this charming ruling:

> *And the parties having informed the Court that the herein matter has been settled amicably (the Court uses the word amicably loosely) and that there is no need for a Court ruling on the remaining motions [or] a trial;*
>
> *And such news of an amicable settlement having made this Court happier than a tick on a fat dog because it is otherwise busier than a one-legged cat in a sand box and, quite frankly, would have rather jumped naked off of a twelve-foot stepladder into a five-gallon bucket of porcupines than have presided over a two-week trial of the herein dispute, a trial which, no doubt, would have made the jury more confused than a hungry baby in a topless bar and made the parties and their attorneys madder than mosquitoes in a mannequin factory; IT IS THEREFORE ORDERED AND ADJUDGED [that] the jury trial scheduled herein for July 13, 2011, is hereby CANCELED.*

At his popular legal-humor blog Lowering the Bar, Kevin Underhill rounded up some of his favorite case names from the US court system:

- *Robin Hood v. U.S. Government Banking Industry,* a "nonsensical" racketeering case brought against the government in 2012; case dismissed.

- *Easter Seals National Society for Crippled Children v. Playboy Enterprises,* a landmark copyright case, in which the Supreme Court effectively ruled that Playboy had the right to use video from an Easter Seals telethon in a pornographic movie.

- *United States ex rel. Mayo v. Satan and His Staff,* in which plaintiff Gerald Mayo claimed that "Satan has on numerous occasions caused plaintiff misery and unwarranted threats . . . placed deliberate obstacles in his path [and] deprived him of his constitutional rights"; case dismissed for several reasons including lack of jurisdiction.

- *Batman v. Commissioner,* in which Ray L. Batman and his wife unsuccessfully challenged the Commissioner of the IRS on tax matters.

- *Association of Irritated Residents v. United States Environmental Protection Agency,* in which groups of California residents sued the EPA over air-quality issues. The residents won."

- *Death v. Graves & Co.,* in which the plaitiff, motorcyclist Alan Death, alleged that he'd been struck by the defendant's vehicle. "Maybe my personal favorite so far," Underhill wrote. "It appears that death lived."

There are Olympic athletes, Olympic trainers, and naturally Olympic lawyers—and like everyone else involved with the famous games, they are relentless in the pursuit of victory.

That's what the organizers of Georgia's "Redneck Olympics" found out when they announced their own grand competition, which features such traditional athletic events as:

- *The cigarette flip*

- *Bobbing for pig trotters*

- *Seed spitting*

- *Toilet-seat throwing*

- *Big-hair contest*

- *Armpit serenade*

- *Bug zapping*

- *Dumpster diving*

- *Hubcap hurling*

The Redneck Olympians soon got a "cease and desist" letter from the U.S. Olympic Committee, which insisted that it owns the word "Olympic," and that the Redneck Olympics could "cause confusion" or "falsely suggest a connection" with officially-sanctioned Olympic activities.

Such confusion may seem unlikely, but rather than responding like rednecks—by, say, using their four-wheelers to churn the U.S. Olympic Committee's front yard into mud—the organizers dutifully changed the name to the Redneck Games, and the games, happily, went on.

—JONATHANTURLEY.ORG

Just out of law school and dressed in a conservative white shirt, gray pants and tie, I was rushing off to court when I was stopped by an elderly woman.

"Are you one of those Latter-day Saints boys on a mission?"

"No ma'am," I said. "I'm an attorney."

"Oh," she said. "You're playing for the other team."

—KEITH POGUE

"Man with 8 DUIs Blames Drinking Problem"

—TAMPA BAY TIMES

A young executive stomped into the elevator, obviously upset. "What's the matter?" asked a business man standing there.

"Nepotism!" shouted the first man. "My boss just bypassed me and made his nephew office manager!"

"I see," the other said, handing over his business card. "If you need legal advice, please call me."

The young man glanced at the card: "O'Brien, O'Brien, O'Brien and O'Brien, Attorneys at Law."

—NORMAN F. PIHALY

Order in the court

There was a notice that appeared in my mailbox. It told me I was required to go to court as a witness against someone whose name I did not recognize. Calling for more information, I found out my notice was for reporting a driver who had illegally passed my stopped school bus—ten years ago when I had been driving a bus part time.

The appearance date was the same time as my night class, so I called to see if my court appearance could be rescheduled. Two days later someone returned my call.

"We cannot push the date back," they said. The reason? "The accused is entitled to a speedy trial."

—JANIS SMITH

The U.S. Chamber Institute for Legal Reform believes that America faces a "legal crisis" of frivolous lawsuits in which lawyers "exploit flaws" and "bankrupt companies" in search of "jackpot justice." Among its examples of absurd lawsuits which was published in 2012:

- *A Florida driver, found guilty of killing three people while driving drunk, sued the deceased driver's estate, claiming he caused the accident.*

- *A Michigan woman demanded $5 million in damages in a class-action suit to repay her for the value of the gas that was in her car when it was repossessed.*

- *An inmate who entered prison with just five teeth sued his jailers for bad dental work.*

Said the Institute's president: "Abuse of our legal system is no joke." Maybe, ma'am, maybe . . . but if that's true, why are we laughing?

Lawyer: Doctor, did you say he was shot in the woods?

A: No. I said he was shot in the lumbar region.

—TRIPOD.COM

On her way home from dinner and drinks, Melanie Shaker of Chicago got angry with her husband and tried to kick him. She missed and smashed the window of a beauty salon, leaving herself a bloody mess.

Naturally, she sued the salon. Part of her argument: the salon should have had stronger glass in its windows, because it sits near Wrigley Field, home of baseball's Chicago Cubs, on a street "frequently traveled by intoxicated pedestrians," which is lawyer-speak for "staggering drunks."

As one expert noted, the woman may find some support in an 1855 Supreme Court decision—Robinson v. Pioche—ruling in favor of a drunk who fell down a hole in a city street. "A drunken man is as much entitled to a safe street as a sober one," the court noted, "and much more in need of it."

—JONATHANTURLEY.ORG

"Florida Reporter Completes Sentence"

—EDITOR AND PUBLISHER

"Why do you want to divorce your wife?" demands the judge.

"Because every night she whispers in my ear: 'It's time for you to go home.'"

—FERENCE L.

SUING IN THE RAIN

You may recall the Washington, D.C., judge who, two years ago, filed a $67 million lawsuit against a dry cleaner for allegedly losing a pair of his pants. Now, in that fine tradition, comes Nello Balan, who sued a Rothschild and a supermodel for $1 million over the loss of an umbrella.

It all began on April 25, 2007, when a model named Le Call dined at Balan's Manhattan restaurant, Nello. When she left, it was raining. Since supermodels have been known to wither in such conditions, the restaurateur kindly lent her an umbrella. Not the cheap kind, manufactured to break at first gust. No, this one was leather. A gift from fashion designer Jean Paul Gaultier, it was valued at $5,000.

Cut to a month later, and the umbrella is AWOL. A quick call to Le Call revealed that she'd lent it to Nathaniel Rothschild, the future fifth Baron Rothschild. But when Rothschild's chauffeur returned the umbrella, it was in two pieces, matching Balan's emotional state upon seeing his beloved umbrella.

Balan eventually lowered his demand to $30,000. But even that was too much for the judge, who tossed water on the umbrella suit and fined Balan's lawyer $500 for filing a frivolous claim.

—READER'S DIGEST

Lawyer: Now, Darren, remember all your responses must be oral. OK?

Lawyer: What school do you go to?

A: Oral.

Lawyer: How old are you?

A: Oral.

—TRIPOD.COM

Dumb v. stupid

We all know that Americans hate lawyers, but we love lawsuits, especially the crazy ones. Even prisoners like to get in on the act. Two prisoners from the maximum-security section of Colorado's Pueblo County Jail slid open their defective cell doors, collected bedsheets and mattress covers from other inmates, and headed to the showers. There they pried off a broken ceiling tile and climbed into a vent, which led them to the roof via a door that was latched from the inside. Once on the roof, the prisoners, Scott Anthony Gomez Jr. and Oscar Mercado, tied the sheets and mattress covers together into a makeshift rope, secured it to a gas pipe, and began to rappel down the northwest side of the jail.

That's when the Great Escape of '07 went to hell in a handbasket. Gomez slipped and fell 40 feet, injuring himself; he was rushed to the hospital, and Mercado was caught soon after.

So how did Gomez while away the hours during his recovery? By filing a lawsuit against the county board of commissioners, sheriff, and guards—for as much as the law would allow—on the grounds that they made it too easy for him to escape. He should know, since this was his second attempt. In his suit, Gomez claimed that the cell doors opened too easily and that guards vacated their posts and ignored information that a jailbreak was nigh. They were practically begging him to break out, he insisted. And who was he to disappoint?

"The defendants knew or should have known that the jail was not secure," read his complaint. "Furthermore, defendants knew that the plaintiff had a propensity to escape."

Gomez couldn't escape the fact that he didn't have a case, which the judge tossed out last September.

—READER'S DIGEST

The Whole Truth and Nothing but the Truth

Lawyers like to share the story about the attorney who was about to ask something really dumb, but stopped himself just in time, saying, "Your honor, I'd like to strike the next question." These other pettifoggers should have followed his example:

- *How many times have you committed suicide?*

- *Were you alone or by yourself?*

- *Do you have any children or anything of that kind?*

- *Without saying anything, tell the jury what you did next.*

- *Was it you or your brother who was killed?*

- *Was that the same nose you broke as a child?*

- *Now, doctor, isn't it true that when a person dies in his sleep, he doesn't know about it until the next morning?*

- *You don't know what it was, and you didn't know what it looked like, but can you describe it?*

- *So, you were gone until you returned?*

- *How many autopsies have you performed on dead people?*

- *Did he kill you?*

Counsel: Now, in your report under "foundation" you indicated that there is a minimum of cracking and no signs of settling.

Witness: Yes.

Counsel: When you say there is a "minimum" of cracking, I take it that you did find some cracking.

Witness: No. Because if I said there was no cracking, I would be in court just like this answering some stupid lawyer's questions. So I put minimum in there to cover myself, because somebody is going to find a crack somewhere.

Judge: I could say I would like to shake your hand, but I won't.

—DISORDERLY CONDUCT

While Americans hate lawyers, we love lawsuits, especially the crazy ones.

- *Take the case of the Lodi, California, city employee who accidentally drove a dump truck into Curtis Gokey's parked truck a few years ago. Gokey sued the city, even though he was the one driving the dump truck.*

- *For some injured parties, no law need even be broken before they wield the lawyer card. In Jurupa, California, a retired Navy Reserve captain threatened to sue her colleagues on the school board if they didn't start addressing her by her military title. And a while back, a father took his son's Little League coach to court over a losing season. And that's just the start.*

—READER'S DIGEST

ePay Up

Ask Steve Shellhorn and he'll probably tell you that if you have nothing nice to say about someone, lie. Shellhorn, a Seattle native, bought coins on eBay from Charles Burgess, who then asked for feedback, a regular practice on the site. Was the service good or bad? Shellhorn was torn. The Morgan silver dollars were in fine shape, and the price was fair. But the packaging left a lot to be desired.

"The coins were hanging out of the envelope," he later told Seattle's King 5 News. There should have been proper packing to keep them in place. With that in mind, Shellhorn left neutral feedback, neither good nor bad.

The lukewarm response got a hot one from Burgess. Charging "fraud" and "extortion," he sued Shellhorn for $10,000 over his "childish and vindictive" behavior, which, he feared, could harm future sales.

Disposition Misery loves company, and Shellhorn had plenty. It turns out that Burgess made it a habit to go after less-than-thrilled customers. The judge sided with Shellhorn but not before he'd spent $500 for an attorney.

—READER'S DIGEST

DUMB
AROUND
THE WORLD

There's something oddly comforting about pulling the camera back to look at

DUMB ON A GLOBAL SCALE.

Suddenly, most of the strange and scary world looks remarkably familiar:

Dumb bosses and workers? Check.

Silly governments and grumpy bureaucrats? Check.

Cocktails made with human body parts? Check.

It really is true: we're a lot more alike than we are different.

That doesn't mean we're identical, of course. Some things that look dumb to us look quite smart to the people of other nations. In Japan, for example, one restaurant offers an entire menu of food made with dirt (including dirt soup, dirt salad, dirt risotto with sea bass, and dirt ice cream for dessert). One local review called the results "divine" and "refreshing," but it's hard to picture Americans lining up for that sort of treat.

And in South Korea, entrepreneurs recently opened a large museum complex—the "Restroom Cultural Park"—that celebrates indoor plumbing with a building shaped like a—well, just guess. Your average American probably uses the throne as much as your average Korean, but it seems unlikely that a toilet-shaped toilet museum will crop up stateside anytime soon.

So we're not all the same. Not all of us all name our businesses after genocidal maniacs.

Not all of us attack our neighbors with sharpened palm fronds over coconut tree disputes.

But anyone, anywhere can end up looking pretty silly when things don't go as planned:

> *Like the Russian airline attendant who took a picture of herself giving the finger to her passengers, and posted it on her country's equivalent of Facebook. Her bosses at Aeroflot weren't amused, and she lost her job.*

> *Like the Polish man who wanted to help with the laundry and watch the fights on TV at the same time. He ended up burning half his face when he answered a hot iron instead of the phone. "I was really getting involved in the boxing and was not really thinking about what I was doing," he said later.*

> *Like the Englishman who couldn't stop fighting with his brother Terry over who should live in the family house—so he smashed it to rubble with a sledgehammer. "I did what I had to do," he said. "Terry's going to be quite bitter."*

Stories like these are a nice reminder of the simple fact of stupid: dumb doesn't care who you are, where you're from, what language you speak, or what religion you follow. It doesn't care if you're big or small, young or old, rich or poor. Whether you live in penthouse or a mud hut, dumb will happily walk through your door—all you have to do is open it.

So join us on a tour of dumb around the world—and don't worry about bringing a translator or a dictionary. Stupid, you'll discover, is a universal language.

Turkey

Customs officials at Antalya airport found themselves squarely in the crosshairs of the global laugh machine after they stamped the passport of a pink stuffed unicorn.

The supposed unicorn was, in reality, a nine-year-old girl from Wales who mistakenly gave the Turkish officials a "Design-A-Bear" passport. It featured a handsome gold-embossed teddy bear on the cover and a photo of a unicorn in a polka-dot overalls inside.

But officials waved the girl through anyway, and the family only later noticed the mistake. "There was a moment of panic when I thought someone would come chasing after us, but nothing," the girl's mother said. "And to make it worse, the unicorn wasn't even on holiday with us."

—DAILYMAIL.CO.UK

Estonia

European officials arrested a gang of smugglers who pumped thousands of gallons of cheap vodka out of Russia and into neighboring Estonia through a mile-long underwater pipeline. The incentive: vodka is heavily taxed in Estonia, but dirt cheap in Russia.

The smugglers managed to pump about 1,600 gallons through the 1.2-mile pipe before getting busted. But their biggest problem was sales—Estonians are discriminating drinkers, and unsurprisingly, pipeline vodka isn't what you'd call top quality.

—SOURCE: TELEGRAPH.CO.UK

Spain

If your dog accidentally leaves his poop on the street in the town of Brunete, never fear! You'll get it back. Just be ready to sign for a package.

Fed up with sidewalk minefields, local leaders adopted an unusual plan. Volunteer poop-spotters would walk the streets looking for owners who don't scoop. They would casually strike up a conversation, find out the dog's name, check it against the national database of registered pets, and ship the poop back to the owner's address.

Sounds crazy, but in one week alone, the town shipped almost one hundred fifty fragrant care packages, and dog-poop levels have dropped in town by 70 percent. That's more effective than their last stunt—a remote-controlled plastic pile-of-poop-on-wheels that would chase non-scooping dog owners down the street.

—SOURCE: TELEGRAPH.CO.UK

Chile

When you're literally making money, typos aren't easily fixed. That's why the head of Chile's national mint lost his job.

Nobody saw the mistake at first, but about a year after a new fifty-peso coin was released, someone finally noticed that instead of "Republica de Chile," it read, "Republica de Chiie."

In the end, a handful of mint workers got fired, including the boss. But recalling thousands of coins isn't cheap—so they're still out there.

—SOURCE: BBC NEWS

Russia

Russia's former minister of finance, Alexei Kudrin, knows a way to generate taxes and goose his country's sluggish economy: Everyone should drink and smoke more.

"Those who drink, those who smoke are doing more to help the state," he said.

—SOURCE: TELEGRAPH.CO.UK

Authorities recently arrested a forty-year-old man in a remote Russian city for stealing a road.

The road, outside the city of Syktyvkar in the heavily forested Komi Republic, was made of large concrete slabs. The thief used heavy machinery to lift 82 of the slabs, worth a total of about $6,000, onto three trucks. He didn't get far.

But lucky for him, he only faced a two-year sentence. These days, political protestors in Russia are looking at much steeper penalties—better to steal a road, apparently, than criticize the government.

—SOURCE: EN.RIA.RU

A villager in the Ural Mountains called police at 3 a.m. recently to report a tank invasion.

Police arrived in the village of Beryozovo to find a 14-ton armored all-terrain vehicle that had run off the road, flattened a garage, and come just short of crushing a woman's house.

Fortunately, despite what some neighbors feared, war had not broken out. But at least one gentleman had gotten very, very drunk. That would be the tank driver, who told police the next morning that he had no idea how he'd gotten to the village.

—SOURCE: BUZZFEED.COM

Denmark

Fishermen in Øresund Sound (between Sweden and Denmark) recently reported a new fish in their catch—the pacu, a piranha look-alike whose favorite dish happens to be between a gentleman's legs.

"It normally eats nuts, fruit, and small fish," one Danish expert said, "but human testicles are just a natural target."

The fish is native to South America and was probably dumped in the Øresund by accident, but it's not impossible that more are out there. "Keep your swimsuit on in the sound these days," the expert said. "It's not normal to get your testicles bitten off, of course, but it can happen."

—SOURCE: TELEGRAPH.CO.UK

When workers at a grocery store in Copenhagen took delivery on their latest batch of bananas, they noticed something funny—some boxes were quite a bit heavier than others.

It wasn't extra fruit: the boxes were packed with 220 pounds of cocaine.

A few days later, workers in at least one store ended up finding bricks of coke in their bananas, which had been shipped from Colombia. Store officials rushed to assure shoppers that the bananas were perfectly safe, but there are probably at least a few customers who wouldn't mind if their fruit came with a little extra kick.

—SOURCE: DAILYCALLER.COM

China

A woman in Beijing recently sued a hotel for failing to wake her up. She overslept and missed an exam, so she demanded over $6,000 in damages.

Unfortunately, 27-year-old Zhao Lin never got to make her case in court; she slept through the court date. That left the hotel managers feeling vindicated: "As we can all see today, she seems to have a problem waking up," said one.

—SOURCE: CROATIANTIMES.COM

Among the popular attractions in the Wuhan city zoo was a talkative mynah bird whose vocabulary included such charming phrases as "hello," "goodbye," and "good fortune."

But mynahs hear everything—and they don't forget. One day the mynah suddenly began spouting obscenities at everyone in earshot, and it had to be quickly escorted away from the paying guests.

Nobody knew quite what had happened. "Maybe some tourist taught the bird this bad language," said zookeeper Li Yun. No matter the reason, the zoo couldn't let its other mynahs get in on the act. The foul mouthed bird was sent to solitary confinement, where it was sentenced to mend its ways by listening to hours and hours of tapes of polite conversation.

—SOURCE: ANIMALNEWYORK.COM

Chinese visitors to an ancient temple in Egypt were shocked to see words in their own language carved in the 3,500-year-old walls: "Ding Jihao was here."

It turned out to be fresh graffiti left by an enterprising fifteen-year-old from Jiangsu Province. Word spread fast, and profuse apologies quickly followed from the boy, his family, and Chinese authorities. Officials have now launched a campaign to encourage their compatriots to be respectful and considerate travelers.

And with more Chinese seeing new countries than ever before, it's likely that the world will learn quickly to accommodate them in spite of the occasional dumb teenager. In 2012, 80 million Chinese spent more than $100 billion, making them the highest-spending tourists in the world.

—SOURCE: DAILYMAIL.CO.UK

Pakistan

Every year since 1992, two zookeepers at Islamabad's Marghazar Zoo have demanded a large annual delivery of alcohol, which they said they used to "calm down" the zoo's elephants during mating season.

"I serve two bottles of vodka to each of the elephants every night from November to February," one zookeeper said. "If we delay giving them booze, they get angry." Every year the zookeepers asked for a bigger ration, telling zoo officials that the elephants would get dangerous without it.

It took only 20 years for someone to ask a veterinarian if elephants drink. The answer: of course not. The alcohol was going exactly where you think it went: down the zookeepers' gullets. Both lost their jobs, but it was a good run while it lasted.

—SOURCE: ISHTIAQRAO.BLOGSPOT.COM

Sweden

The woman convicted of assaulting a bus driver with a banana won't have to pay $1,000 in damages.

That doesn't mean she's off the hook completely—the conviction for banana assault still stands. By the driver's telling, it was a brutal, unprovoked attack that injured his retina: "She hit me right in the face with the half-eaten banana. I had banana all over me—on my tie, my shirt, and my eye."

The woman, however, argued that the driver almost hit her car, and that when she entered the bus to rationally discuss the matter, the banana slipped.

The court may not have believed that, but it did believe her when she argued that it was "unreasonable that a banana could cause this much damage." They reduced her penalty to about $100.

—SOURCE: THELOCAL.SE

It's true what they say about Scandinavia: it's just plain civilized.

Take the case of the forgetful jailers at Norrtälje prison, near Stockholm. On a recent Friday night, they forgot to lock up six inmates, including three convicted murderers.

So what did the thugs do with their remarkable chance? They baked a sticky Swedish chocolate cake called a *kladdkaka* and watched TV. "The coziest evening we've had in a long time," said one.

—SOURCE: JULIAMOVED.COM

Canada

A traveler in Winnipeg reported this exchange with a fussy server in a sit-down restaurant:

Me: Could my daughter get a baked potato instead of the fries, please?

Waitress: No.

Me: No? Why? Are you out of baked potatoes?

Waitress: No, but we've only got a few, and we're saving them for the adult customers. Kids prefer fries anyway.

Me: She loves baked potatoes! Are you seriously not going to let her have one?

Waitress: Nope!

—NOTALWAYSWORKING.COM

Key West has the margarita. In Munich, Germany, it's the frothy stein of beer. And for one town deep in Canada's Yukon Territory, the signature drink is a cocktail made with a human toe.

They call it the Sourtoe, and since its invention in 1973, more than six hundred thousand visitors to Dawson City's Sourdough Saloon have knocked one back. If your lips touch the toe—eight of which have been donated over the years by various unfortunates who've lost them to frostbite, diabetes, inoperable corns, and a lawn mower accident— you become a member in good standing of the Sourtoe Cocktail Club.

Any drink will do, as long as there's a toe in it.

And while at least one toe has been swallowed, the safely preserved (but truly ugly) digits haven't hurt anyone yet. They've also done wonders for the remote town's reputation. "It's hard to become famous," said the Sourtoe's inventor, Dick Stevenson. "It's much easier to become infamous."

—SOURCE: SOURTOECOCKTAILCLUB.COM

Ireland

They take their rules as seriously on the Emerald Isle as anywhere else. A student reported this exchange in her school cafeteria:

Me: Can I also have two slices of white bread please?

Server: Sorry, we need the white bread to make toast.

Me: So, you won't sell me the white bread as you need to keep it to sell as toast?

Server: YES!

Me: Can I have untoasted toast please?

Server: NO!

—NOTALWAYSWORKING.COM

Wales

An actor in the city of Cardiff reported this exchange between a fellow actor and one of the theater's technical staff.

Actress: So I heard you're Canadian!

Tech Guy: Yes, that's right.

Actress: How'd you get to be that, then?

Tech Guy: Uh, well, I was born there.

Actress: Oh. So where is Canadia [sic], then? Is it near Sweden?

—NOTALWAYSWORKING.COM

England

Bosses can be as dumb in the UK as anywhere else. One fast-food worker from Lancashire reported this conversation:

Manager: Can you stay another four hours?

Me: What? Why?

Manager: Your coworker has drunk some wine, and can't come in.

Me: Isn't it her wedding day today?

Manager: Yes, that's why she's been drinking.

Me: And you scheduled her to work today?

Manager: Yes.

Me: Seriously?

Manager: Yes.

Me: And you didn't think that would be a problem?

Manager: No.

The worker covered for the colleague. No word on whether or not the boss was boiled in oil.

—NOTALWAYSWORKING.COM

"British Left Waffles on Falklands"

—THE GUARDIAN

A seasoned European traveler passed on this story from the days when strikes, global competition and Margaret Thatcher were shaking up Britain's mining industry:

"I was hitchhiking through Yorkshire in 1984 and stopped in a pub for lunch," he recalled. "I sat at the bar where everyone was complaining about Ian MacGregor shutting down the local mine.

"After listening awhile, I innocently asked if there was any coal left. The response was dead silence. Finally one miner said, "The coal ran out a decade ago, but that's beside the point!'"

—GLEN EMERY

A financial institution in London recently decided it wanted to advertise special services to all of its top clients. So the bank came up with a computer program that would scan its database for wealthy customers and automatically send them letters.

Unfortunately, one programmer decided to indulge in a little snark while drafting the letter—and he forgot to correct the draft before the program went live.

You know where this is going: suddenly, the bank's customers started getting letters that read, "Dear Rich Bastard . . ."

—SOURCE: SNOPES.COM

Czech Republic

The official English-language radio news bulletin in Prague recently featured two notable items.

One headline read: "Ministry presents annual awards for promoting the good name of the country."

Just below that: 'Finance Minister Miroslav Kalousek admits being drunk in interviews."

—SOURCES: RADIO PRAGUE, MARK NESSMITH

Ghana

Word to the wise: if you want to prune your neighbor's coconut tree, be sure to wear your iron underwear.

That's what one fisherman in the district of Half Assini wishes he'd done after he tried to trim some branches that overhung his property. Ezah Kojo had climbed the trunk and was ready to saw away when the tree's furious owners—a 48-year-old woman and her daughter—attacked him from below with a large sharpened palm branch.

The two women probably didn't mean to seriously hurt him. But something went badly awry. The stiff frond sunk deep in Kojo's vulnerable rear, and while we'll spare you the gory details, the unlucky fisherman had to be rushed to the hospital and can no longer move his bowels "in the traditional fashion."

The women were found guilty of assault, and while a stern sentence is expected, it seems that the would-be tree trimmer got the worse punishment.

—SOURCE: GHANAWEB.COM

New Zealand

No matter where you go in the world, people talk smack about their neighbors. It's no different in New Zealand, where the prime minister was once asked asked whether he was concerned by the large number of Kiwis moving to nearby Australia.

The late "Piggy" Muldoon's famous reply: "New Zealanders who emigrate to Australia raise the IQ of both countries."

Australia

A customer in a restaurant in Melbourne reported this conversation with an unfortunate worker:

Me: Can I have a toasted ham and cheese sandwich?

Cashier: Umm . . . I 'm not sure. I'll have to see.
(The cashier disappears into the back room, talks to someone, and returns empty-handed.)

Cashier: Sorry, I've got no ham and cheese left. In fact we've got hardly any food. That was my boss I was just talking to. He just told me he's closing the business at the end of today, so I'm officially unemployed in about . . . um . . . three hours. Now I know why we've had no food delivered all week. Actually, I should probably just close now since we've got no food anyway. Sorry to ruin your day!

Me: That's okay. I think someone else just had a worse one.

—NOTALWAYSWORKING.COM

Syria

Anonymous hackers recently broke into the official accounts of President Bashar al-Assad, retrieving hundreds of e-mails and dumping them online for all the world to see.

Among the embarrassing revelations: while you might expect the ruthless dictator to have ironclad online protection, he didn't.

In fact, it was just the opposite: Assad's password was "12345"—what experts call the least-secure password possible.

—SOURCE: TECHDIRT.COM

India

Competition for shoppers in the city of Ahmedabad is stiff, and shop owner Manish Chandani wanted a name that would honor his family and make his clothing store stand out.

So he put a swastika in the sign and called the shop "Hitler."

It's memorable, all right. A small surge of global outrage followed, and Chandani quickly agreed to change the name and logo. "I was not aware of Hitler being responsible for the killing of six million people before the shop's inauguration," he said. "This time I will choose a noncontroversial name."

So how did he hear the name *Hitler* in the first place? It was his "very strict" grandfather's nickname, Chandani said.

—SOURCE: BBC.CO.UK

Cambodia

After forty years of marriage, one couple in Prey Veng Province decided that the time had come to split up—so the husband and friends sawed the house in half.

"It is the strangest thing I've ever seen," a local reporter said. The husband took his half to his parents' property, where he rebuilt it. The wife left hers where it stood. And their two children each got a quarter of the family property.

The only ones who got nothing were the lawyers. "This was a not a legal divorce," one said. "It never went to the court."

—SOURCE: CNN.COM

Hong Kong

A businessman meeting Chinese clients reported this conversation between a friend of his and a lovely young woman at an upscale restaurant in Hong Kong:

Businessman: So, what do you do for a living?

Woman: Me? I'm just a prostitute.

Businessman (mouth dropping open): Uh, wow, that's, um, really interesting. I bet you make lots of money.

Woman: Not really. But that's not even the worst part. The hours are very long, so I'm pulling overtime nearly every single day.

Businessman: Is that so? Well, okay then.

Woman: And don't even get me started on the paperwork.

Businessman: Wait, what?
(At this moment, a second woman leans over and starts whispering in Cantonese. The first woman immediately starts blushing.)

Woman: I'm very sorry for the confusion! I'm a PROSECUTOR. Not . . . what I said earlier.

Businessman: Now that makes sense! Here I am, thinking that you had a really bad pimp or something!

—NOTALWAYSWORKING.COM

"West Point Cadets Train for Life in Iraq with Weekend in N.J."

—*TIMES HERALD-RECORD*

Iran

Government officials in Tehran have infuriated the terrorist organization of Al Qaeda by suggesting that the United States government staged the infamous September 11 attacks in New York City.

Iran's president, Mahmoud Ahmadinejad, suggested in a speech that the official version of events was a "big fabrication," and that the U.S. blew up its own buildings and murdered its own people.

This left Al Qaeda, which spent many years preparing the attacks, feeling grossly insulted. "Why would Iran ascribe to such a ridiculous belief?" one writer said. "[Iran does] not want to give Al Qaeda credit for the greatest and biggest operation ever committed against America."

No word on Iran's theories about the Kennedy assassination or the moon landing.

—TELEGRAPH.CO.UK

Belgium

Europeans know that the French are fond of Belgian jokes, portraying their neighbors as dumb, uncultured, and so on. The Belgians, for their part, have long been hesitant to return fire.

That's why, when the silent French film *The Artist* earned an unprecedented ten Academy Award nominations, this line started making the rounds in Belgium: "When the French shut up, the whole world appreciates them!"

—SOURCE: BLOGS.TRANSPARENT.COM

Brazil

How do you give yourself a leg up in Brazilian politics? Change your name to a variation of Barack Obama. Six candidates in Brazil's local elections recently did just that.

But office seekers didn't stop there. Two hundred renamed themselves after Luiz Inácio Lula da Silva, which just happened to be the name of Brazil's immensely popular president. Other people looking for the public's votes have included a Bill Clinton, a Jorge Bushi, and one Chico Bin Laden.

—TELEGRAPH.CO.UK

Thailand

Law enforcement officials in the capital of Bangkok want to deliver "guilt and shame" to their own officers, and they think "Hello Kitty" is just the ticket.

Under a new initiative, police caught littering, parking illegally, or otherwise disgracing the uniform will be required to wear bright pink armbands adorned with the ubiquitous cartoon kitten, along with a pair of linked hearts.

Not exactly the image any cop wants to project. "Kitty is a cute icon for young girls," said one official. "It's not something macho police officers want covering their biceps."

The new pink armbands quickly made their mark. "The police are scared," an anonymous officer said. "It will be very embarrassing to walk around with Hello Kitty on your arm."

But this extreme policy was only necessary because the plaid armbands they'd been using weren't working—instead of being ashamed, officers were taking them home as souvenirs.

—SOURCE: NEWYORKTIMES.COM

Argentina

In a country famous for its love of both beer and rugby, it should probably be no surprise that someone invented a beer vending machine you have to tackle.

It's called the "Rugbeer machine," and even after you've put inyour money, you have to hit it with a full body blow to get it to release your beer.

No little love taps will do—the machine is happy to make jokes about you if you can't hit it hard enough. And while the manufacturer reports no fatalities yet, it could be just a matter of time. In the United States, at least 37 people have been killed by tipped-over vending machines since 1978.

—SOURCE: ADWEEK.COM

Myanmar

In the country still known to most as Burma, almost every aspect of daily life has long been controlled by a rigid and ruthless dictatorship. Naturally that has included aggressive censorship, run from an office called the Division of Press Scrutiny.

During a recent political thaw, however, that office was shut down for good. The former director, U Tint Swe, said he was glad to be done with an ugly job. "We didn't arrest or torture anyone," he said, "but we had to torture their writing."

—SOURCE: NEWYORKTIMES.COM

CELEBRI-

DUMB

It's not a bad gig, being a
CELEBRITY **IN AMERICA.**

There's lots of work. There's plenty of money. Stay on the right side of public opinion, and life can be a lot of fun.

But do something dumb, and that's when our stars find out what they're really getting paid for. At such moments, if it were legal to put stars in the stocks, half the country would happily head to the town square armed with sacks of rotten vegetables.

The other half would kick back on the couch to watch the show.

We're more civilized now, of course. Often the worst we can do to celebrity screwups is plaster their sorry faces on tabloid covers and TV talk shows—which we do with relish. Because there's something about the dumbstyles of the rich and famous that we find endlessly entertaining. They make gobs of money and blow it. They make terrible relationship decisions over and over again. And they can be hilariously self-centered, weird, and clueless:

> *Like heiress Paris Hilton, who once stated, "No, no, I didn't go to England; I went to London."*

> *Like actor Terrence Howard, who won't keep dating a woman who uses just toilet paper: "If she doesn't make the adjustment to baby wipes, I'll know she's not completely clean."*

> *Like actress Jennifer Aniston, who had such a hard time choosing her new dog from a litter that she named her "Sophie"—in honor of the title character in* Sophie's

Choice, *in which a mother must send one of her two children to die in the Nazi gas chambers. "I was crying," Aniston said. "It was so hard."*

Many of our stars of stage and sport understand that theirs is not an intellectual profession. "I'm a meathead, man," actor Keanu Reeves once said. "You just happen to be spending some time with a dumb person."

And others understand that celebrity can make stupid much worse. Take football star Nate Newton, who made millions playing for the Dallas Cowboys, only to be accused—not once, but twice—of possessing hundreds of pounds of marijuana. He went to jail and came out a wiser man: "We are who we are. Sports don't make us smarter."

Our stars often perform the same role in life as lottery winners: they show us what happens when you combine normal human problems with huge piles of money.

All too often, the results are far from pretty. But that's what we love. If you want to glue us to our screens, give us Charlie Sheen smoking cigarettes through his nose and blowing up his career on live TV: "I am on a drug, it's called Charlie Sheen. It's not available because if you try it once you will die. Your face will melt off and your children will weep over your exploded body."

So enjoy this brief tour of celebrity stupidity. We have much to learn from our stars, and they'll tell us all about it in their own words. They teach us that success doesn't guarantee satisfaction.

And most clearly of all, they teach us that money can't buy brains.

Quotable

"I'd rather smoke crack" than eat cheese from a can.

—ACTRESS GWYNETH PALTROW

"I can't really remember the names of the clubs that we went to."

—BASKETBALL PLAYER SHAQUILLE O'NEAL,
ASKED IF HE'D VISITED THE PARTHENON WHILE IN GREECE

"I think there's a difference between ditzy and dumb. Dumb is just not knowing. Ditzy is having the courage to ask!"

—ACTRESS JESSICA SIMPSON

"I was asked to come to Chicago because Chicago is one of our fifty-two states."

—ACTRESS RAQUEL WELCH

"It was the dumbest thing I've ever done."

—HULK HOGAN ON HANDLING A STEAMING RADIATOR CAP. HE LATER
APOLOGIZED FOR TWEETING GRAPHIC PHOTOS FROM THE EMERGENCY ROOM,
SAYING, "I REALLY SHOULD TAKE A MOMENT BEFORE I MAKE A DECISION."

"What's Walmart? Do they like make walls there?"

—PARIS HILTON

"He treats us like men. He lets us wear earrings."

—COLLEGE FOOTBALL PLAYER TORRIN POLK ON HIS COACH

"The number of lines in your forehead tells how many lives you've lived."

—ACTOR ASHTON KUTCHER

The good news for celebrities who can't stand the constant attention is that it won't last forever.

That fact was proudly on display in the town of Long Branch, New Jersey, where cops got a call about a scruffy old man wandering around the Hispanic neighborhood, acting suspicious.

A 24-year-old officer approached him, and found that the man had no ID. But he told her his name, so she called downtown and asked, "Have any of you ever heard of Bob Dylan?"

"I'm afraid we all fell about laughing," an older officer said later. "If it was me, I'd have been demanding his autograph, not his ID. The poor woman has taken rather a lot of abuse from us. I offered to bring in some of my Dylan albums. Unfortunately, she doesn't know what vinyl is either."

—DAILYMAIL.CO.UK

During halftime of a particularly ugly basketball game, Charles Barkley, the Hall of Fame player and current TV analyst, quipped that a famous coach, Herb Magee, was "rolling over in his grave."

After the game, reporters were able to check up on that possibility, since Magee remains very much alive. Had he heard Barkley's comment? "Yes, I did," the venerable coach said. "I died laughing.'"

—SOURCE: ARTICLES.PHILLY.COM

"If I die before my cat, I want a little of my ashes put in his food so I can live inside him."

—ACTRESS DREW BARRYMORE

"You have to treat Paula like a poodle, one that you've rescued from the pound and who needs attention."

—AMERICAN IDOL JUDGE AND PRODUCER SIMON COWELL,
ON FELLOW JUDGE PAULA ABDUL

CELEBRI-DUMB

Quick on Their Feet

Whether in sport or on screen, creativity is essential to any star's success. That's particularly true for those caught doing the wrong thing in the wrong place at the wrong time. Here are just a few of the more intriguing excuses offered up by celebrities in tight spots:

● *Politician Newt Gingrich, talking about cheating on his wife: "At times of my life, partially driven by how passionately I felt about this country . . . I worked far too hard . . . things happened in my life that were not appropriate."*

—SOURCE: CBSNEWS.COM

● *According to a security guard at the scene, actress Winona Ryder, caught stealing from a department store in Beverly Hills: "A movie director told me to shoplift to prepare for a movie role."*

—SOURCE: DAILYMAIL.CO.UK

● *College football player Antonio Morrison, arrested for barking at a police dog: He insisted that the dog barked at him first. (Charges were dropped.)*

—SOURCE: JONATHANTURKEY.ORG

● *Comedian Eddie Murphy, stopped with a prostitute in his car: "I was being a Good Samaritan. It's not the first hooker I've helped out . . . I'll pull over and I'll empty my wallet out to help."*

—SOURCE: NNDB.COM

Tennis player Lighton Ndefwayl, explaining his loss in a tournament: *"He beat me because my jockstrap was too tight and because when he serves he farts, and that made me lose my concentration."*

—SOURCE: INDEPENDENT.CO.UK

"I've never really wanted to go to Japan. Simply because I don't like eating fish. And I know that's very popular out there in Africa."
—SINGER BRITNEY SPEARS

"I want to rush for 1,000 or 1,500 yards, whichever comes first."
—COLLEGE RUNNING BACK GEORGE ROGERS

"It's really hard to maintain a one-on-one relationship if the other person is not going to allow me to be with other people."
—SINGER AXL ROSE

"Dr. Ruth Talks About Sex with Newspaper Editors"

—RUTLAND HERALD

"I want Brooklyn to be christened, but don't know into what religion yet."
—SOCCER STAR DAVID BECKHAM ON HIS NEWBORN SON

"Well, you can't mess up playing a character you've never seen. I've never really met God face to face, so I was sorta making it up as I went along."
—ACTOR MORGAN FREEMAN, ON PLAYING GOD

How to Survive Celebrity

A little bit of class goes a long way when you're a celebrity. That's what sportswriter Steve Politi found out when he spotted legendary golfer Arnold Palmer drinking the cocktail named for him.

The sight left Politi with one burning question: how does Arnold Palmer order an Arnold Palmer? "It has to be a bit awkward, right?" Politi wrote. "Does he tell the waitress, 'I'll have a me?' Does he just expect that she'll know?"

So the writer chased down the golfer's waitress, who dished. "He leaned over and said, 'I'll have a Mr. Palmer,'" she said. "Then he winked."

"My show is the stupidest show on TV. If you are watching it, get a life."

—TALK SHOW HOST JERRY SPRINGER

"I'm not a nest-egg person."

—SINGER ELTON JOHN, AFTER COURT PROCEEDINGS REVEALED HE HAD RACKED UP OVER $2 MILLION IN BILLS EVERY MONTH FOR AN EXTENDED PERIOD

"If only faces could talk."

—FOOTBALL BROADCASTER AND HALL OF FAME PLAYER PAT SUMMERALL

"Fiction writing is great. You can make up almost anything."

—IVANA TRUMP

"If I go down, I'm going down standing up."

—NBA PLAYER CHUCK PERSON

"My sister's expecting a baby, and I don't know if I'm going to be an uncle or an aunt."

—COLLEGE BASKETBALL PLAYER CHUCK NEVITT

"They X-rayed my head and found nothing."

—BASEBALL PLAYER DIZZY DEAN, AFTER BEING HIT BY A BASEBALL

"The word *genius* isn't applicable in football. A genius is a guy like Norman Einstein."

—NFL QUARTERBACK JOE THEISMANN

"The only happy artist is a dead artist, because only then you can't change. After I die, I'll probably come back as a paintbrush."

—ACTOR/DIRECTOR SYLVESTER STALLONE

"There is certainly more in the future now than back in 1964."

—SINGER ROGER DALTREY

"We've got to pause and ask ourselves: how much clean air do we need?"

—AUTO EXECUTIVE LEE IACOCCA, ONE-TIME CEO OF THE CHRYSLER CORP.

All's Fair in Love and Celebrity

Celebrity train-wreck marriages are a dime a dozen, but few are more absurd than the union of NBA player Kris Humphries and reality TV star Kim Kardashian. Massively hyped from the start, the run-up to the marriage included a two-day TV special called *Kim's Fairytale Wedding* and the release of a new perfume called Love, by Kim Kardashian.

Sadly for those who believe in true love, the marriage lasted only 72 days. Here are some things that lasted longer:

- *A season of* American Idol: *119 days.*

- *O. J. Simpson's murder trial: 253 days.*

- *Lifespan of an adult American cockroach: 365 days.*

—SOURCE: BUZZFEED.COM

"We all get heavier as we get older because there's a lot more information in our heads."

——NBA PLAYER VLADE DIVAC

"In the early 80s, I was pretty innocent and confused. I was like Marie Osmond, only with bigger hair and lashes."

—SINGER BOY GEORGE

"Chemistry is a class you take in high school or college, where you figure out two plus two is 10, or something."

——NBA STAR DENNIS RODMAN

"Is this chicken what I have, or is this fish? I know it's tuna but it says 'Chicken by the Sea.'"

—ACTRESS JESSICA SIMPSON

Admit it: you want to know what famous people really smell like, but you never thought to ask. Never fear! Writer Elon Green of TheAwl.com combed through dozens of stories and interviews to see how the scents of the rich and famous have been described in black and white:

- *Jazz trumpeter Miles Davis: "chicken soup."*

- *Shock DJ Howard Stern: "death."*

- *Singer Steven Tyler: "a skunk."*

- *Director Steven Spielberg: "a newborn baby."*

- *Singer Taylor Swift: "expensive wood."*

- *Actor Kevin Bacon: "a little mix of baby powder and Listerine."*

- *Actress Anne Hathaway: "nachos and maple syrup."*

- *Actor Matthew Fox: "a liquor cabinet."*

- *Reality TV star Snooki: "King Kong's you-know-what."*

"I'm so naive about finances. Once when my mother mentioned an amount and I realized that I didn't understand she had to explain: 'That's like three Mercedes.' Then I understood."

—ACTRESS BROOKE SHIELDS

"I enjoy the company of cattle. I really enjoy knowing them, running my hand over them."

—ACTOR RUSSELL CROWE

"I never was asked, Did you see her in person?"

—MANTI TE'O, NORTRE DAME FOOTBALL STAR TO KATIE COURIC ABOUT LENNAY
KEKUA, WITH WHOM HE'D CLAIMED TO HAVE AN ONLINE RELATIONSHIP

"Sources Tell ABC News' Jon Karl Obama Will Be Buried At Sea"

—ABCWORLDNEWS.COM

"They already live off the government and now they're having more kids?"

—COMEDIAN HARI KONDABOLU,
ON THE BIRTH OF ENGLAND'S LATEST ROYAL BABY, PRINCE GEORGE

"I've been fortunate—I haven't had too many auditions. I slept with the right people."

—ACTRESS PAMELA ANDERSON

"I'm not going for the Sixteenth Chapel."

—SINGER JUSTIN BEIBER, AFTER BEING TOLD THAT TOO
MANY TATTOOS COULD LEAVE HIM LOOKING LIKE
MICHELANGELO'S FAMOUS ART IN THE SISTINE CHAPEL

"Yo, I failed ninth grade three times, but I don't think it was necessarily 'cause I'm stupid."

—RAPPER EMINEM

"You guys are just standing up because you feel bad that I fell, and that's really embarrassing, but thank you."

—ACTRESS JENNIFER LAWRENCE, AFTER SHE STUMBLED ONSTAGE
TO ACCEPT THE ACADEMY AWARD FOR BEST ACTRESS

Cyclist Lance Armstrong was the toast of the sporting world for years, winning seven Tour de France titles and raising millions for charity. That all collapsed when a long investigation finally proved what had long been whispered: Armstrong had cheated all along with steroids and banned performance-enhancing drugs.

That prompted one Australian library to post this sign:

"ALL NONFICTION LANCE ARMSTRONG BOOKS, INCLUDING *Lance Armstrong: Images of a Champion, The Lance Armstrong Performance Program* and *Lance Armstrong: World's Greatest Champion* WILL SOON BE MOVED TO THE FICTION SECTION."

—NEATORAMA.COM

Diva Alert!

When bands go on tour, they routinely give venues what are known as "tour riders," describing the artists' requirements for a good show. Typically that includes food and drinks and a variety of special requests, some of which make sense, and some of which seem a little . . . picky:

- *Singer Ne-Yo requires a medium-bristle toothbrush and, "for cleaning a bottle of Ketel One vodka."*

- *The band BoyzIIMen requires roses with ""NO thorns and NO leafs [sic]" and no "FISH WITH WHISKERS."*

- *Singer Katy Perry's 45-page rider demanded a dressing room draped in "cream or soft pink," two "egg chairs" (one with a footstool), ("ABSOLUTELY NO CARNATIONS," and a limo driver who "WILL NOT START A CONVERSATION" or "STAIR [sic] AT THE BACKSEAT THRU THE REARVIEUW [sic] MIRROR."*

- *Singer Janet Jackson prohibits jokes about herself or the Jackson family.*

- *Veteran rockers Duran Duran have obviously gained some appreciation for fine wine over the years, requiring "3 bottles of excellent quality Italian red wine—Sassicaia, Solaia or Tignanello—vintages between '89 and '97" and "2 bottles of excellent quality white wine—Corton-Charlemagne preferred—vintages 1996, 1999, 2001, 2002, 2004."*

- *Oversize singer Meat Loaf, who had collapsed on stage, required two oxygen tanks and "two (2) local EMTs . . . to administer oxygen and/or care as needed . . . THIS IS A MUST."*

"You can expect Bobby to be Bobby. If Bobby ain't Bobby, Bobby just can't be Bobby."

—SINGER BOBBY BROWN

"It's not the most intellectual job in the world, but I do have to know the letters."

—GAME SHOW HOSTESS VANNA WHITE
ON HER ROLE ON *WHEEL OF FORTUNE*

"Don't bother. It's totally not worth watching."

—ACTRESS NICOLE RICHIE, ON HER SHOW *THE SIMPLE LIFE*

"It's a drag having to wear socks during matches, because the tan, like, stops at the ankles. I can never get my skin, like, color coordinated."

—TENNIS STAR MONICA SELES

"I went up there, and I just went blank. So, I bent down, licked his hand and went off."

—ACTRESS BRIDGET MOYNAHAN ON MEETING THE POPE

"I love British cinema like a doctor loves his dying patient."

—ACTOR BEN KINGSLEY

Nobody has spent more time cultivating an image than Martha Stewart—and nobody has poked more holes in it than her own daughter. Here are choice selections from Alexis Stewart's book about life with and without the queen of the happy home:

- *"She used to have me wrap my own presents. She would hand me things right before Christmas and say, 'Now wrap these, but don't look inside.'"*

- *"There were no costumes [at Halloween]. There was no anything. We turned off all the lights and pretended we weren't home."*

- *"There was never anything to eat at my house. Other people had food. I had no food . . . There were ingredients but no prepared food of any kind."*

Stewart didn't let the dirty laundry bother her, calling the book "hilarious" and urging her fans to open their wallets. "I encourage you to buy it, read it, and make it a bestseller."

"I think God is a giant vibrator in the sky . . . a pulsating force of incredible energy."

—ACTOR DAVID ARQUETTE

"That's why I don't eat friggin' lobster. Because they're alive when you kill it."

—PERFORMER SNOOKI,
FROM THE REALITY SERIES *JERSEY SHORE*

"Right now, I'm trying to just finish my record and get through the last season of *Gossip Girl.* So not so much thinking about that."

—ACTRESS TAYLOR MOMSEN, WHEN ASKED WHAT SHE WAS
DOING TO HELP HAITI AFTER A DEVASTATING EARTHQUAKE

"Don't pass me the ball when I'm open—it makes me nervous."

—NBA PLAYER KWAME BROWN, TO TEAMMATE KOBE BRYANT

In a 2013 interview with the Daily Beast, Hollywood legend Billy Sammeth dished about managing big time stars.

On managing Joan Rivers for years: "I hate to besmirch the reputation of an innocent dog, but a lot of time her personality is like a rabid pit bull."

On doing the same job for Cher: "You know when you're four or five years old and you're holding the leash of a German shepherd and the dog is dragging you down the street but you think that you're in control because you're holding the leash? That's what managing Cher was like."

On tangling with Donald Trump: "He goes, 'You know who would have been a great booking for *Celebrity Apprentice,* and the network wouldn't allow it? O. J. Simpson.' I thought to myself, you are now finished in my book."

THEDAILYBEAST.COM

"'At Last' Singer Etta James Dies"

—RICHMOND TIMES-DISPATCH

"He doesn't really take off his clothes. I've never seen Hef naked."

—PLAYBOY PLAYMATE CRYSTAL HARRIS, CURRENT WIFE OF HUGH HEFNER

"It's more than a pleasure to be here tonight. In fact, it's a damn inconvenience."

—CARTOONIST BIL KEANE, CREATOR OF *THE FAMILY CIRCUS,*
HOSTING CARTOONING'S ANNUAL REUBEN AWARDS

"I know for a fact it's not in my destiny to die listening to a Britney Spears album, so I always put that on in my [headphones] when I'm flying."

—ACTRESS MEGAN FOX

"A lot of the men on my mother's side of the family had the middle name Woodbury, and about ten years ago we asked my grandfather where it came from, and he said that when he was born in Gardiner, Maine, in 1904, his mother thought that the town drunk was the funniest guy she'd ever met, and his name was Woodbury. So we're all named after not just a drunk, but a jolly turn-of-the-century drunk."

—TV PRODUCER SETH MACFARLANE,
CREATOR OF *FAMILY GUY* AND CO-CREATOR OF *AMERICAN DAD!*

"I owe a lot to my parents, especially my mother and father."

—GOLFER GREG NORMAN

CELEBRI-DUMB

"One thing I learned from drinking is that if you ever go Christmas caroling, you should go with a group of people. And also go in mid-December."

—LOUIS C. K.

Out of the Mouths of Celebrities

According to Andy Simmons, our humor editor here at _Reader's Digest,_ celebrities are pros at providing lame excuses. In case you're ever in need of a quick excuse to wriggle out of an awkward situation, Andy has provided a starter script just for you.

Yes, sir, it's true that the words _big, fat idiot_ were preceded by the words _you are a._ However, I assure you my words were "taken out of context."[1] But "I apologize if my comments offended."[2] "The truth is, I'm not perfect. This is not about perfection."[3] I understand that our harsh words stem from the fact that I neglected to get you the contract this morning. But "I had other priorities."[4] Last night, I was busy with a friend. No, we don't have to tell my wife—"I was just giving her a ride home,"[5] that's all. But after what happened, HR insisted that I take a certain test, and well, I didn't pass, you know, because of my "vanishing twin."[6] I believe I told you all about that. No? My bad. But I swear "I didn't inhale and never tried it again."[7] And no, there is nothing suspicious about those pills security found. I need them. "I have really bad menstrual cramps."[8] Yes, I'm aware that I'm a man: I suffer sympathy cramps. Besides, I also need them because "I have severe acid reflux."[9] The police weren't convinced either. Then again, "the police, since my trouble, have not worked out for me."[10] But not to worry, I'll get that contract to you just as soon as my trial ends. No, I'm not sure when that will be, since "I didn't show up for court, because I didn't have a professional bodyguard."[11]

1. *Russell Crowe's representative, after Crowe implied that Sharon Stone had had a face-lift and looked like a chimpanzee*

2. *Kentucky senator Jim Bunning's non-apology after saying that Supreme Court justice Ruth Bader Ginsburg would not survive her cancer*

3. *Laurie David, green queen and producer of* An Inconvenient Truth, *after it was revealed that she'd flown several times on a carbon-spewing private jet*

4. *Dick Cheney on why he avoided serving in Vietnam*

5. *Eddie Murphy, after he was pulled over by cops for picking up a transvestite prostitute*

6. *Olympic cyclist Tyler Hamilton explaining away blood-doping charges. He claims his twin sibling died in utero, so he has two kinds of blood in his body.*

7. *Bill Clinton on his attempt at smoking pot*

8. *Nicole Richie explaining why Vicodin was in her system after she was found driving the wrong way on a freeway*

9. *Ashlee Simpson, after she was caught lip-synching on* Saturday Night Live

10. *O.J. Simpson on why he didn't call the police to help him retrieve his stolen goods from a Las Vegas hotel room*

11. *Courtney Love on why she failed to appear for her hearing on a drug-possession charge*

HI-TECH
DUMB

Let's face it:

NOTHING IS AS DUMB AS THE INTERNET.

Which is pretty strange, considering the brainpower behind it. Millions and millions of hours of intense labor by some of the most intelligent people in the world have combined to produce a communication network unparalleled in human experience. Things we once saw only in movies—video phones, touch screens, instantaneous digital transmission across massive distances—we now see every day.

In fact, just about the only thing the Internet can't give us is a decent flying car.

So what do we do with this incredible technology? We do the stupidest stuff imaginable. At the popular social networking site Reddit, one user posed a question:

If someone from the 1950s suddenly appeared . . . what would be the most difficult thing to explain about life today?

Among the top-rated answers:

I possess a device, in my pocket, that is capable of accessing the entirety of information known to man. I use it to look at pictures of cats and get in arguments with strangers.

Admit it: if you've used the Internet, you've used it for dumb stuff. You've looked at silly pictures. You've forwarded terrible jokes. You've wasted hours and hours and hours and hours. According to one recent survey from the Pew Internet and

American Life Project, three-quarters of the people who go online use the Internet "just for fun." They're goofing around, and so are you.

At one point or another, you've probably felt kind of bad about this. You were watching videos of skateboarding dogs and falling-down brides when you should have been working or cleaning or picking up your mother at the airport. You felt pretty stupid yourself. "How could I have gotten so distracted?" you ask. "Why was it so important to me to click on just one . . . more . . . link?"

Relax: science has the answer. It turns out that you're just trying to survive.

Our brains are wired to deliver bursts of chemical pleasure when we discover new stuff. It's an evolutionary thing. Back in our caveman days, the people with best chance of survival were the ones willing to look under every single rock to see if there was anything tasty to eat—or anything nasty that needed killing.

People who didn't look under every rock either missed some meals or turned into meals themselves.

So we all ended up with these busy brains—and then along comes the Internet, which is like an endless room full of boxes marked, "Surprise inside!" Once we walk into that room, we find it biologically impossible to stop opening the boxes. And even if what's inside is really stupid, it's the thrill of the hunt that grabs us.

So next time you kill off an afternoon online, remember, you're not being dumb—you're protecting the species.

But likewise, be sure to watch your step. Whether you're texting or sharing or talking to the tech-support guys about how your computer's cup holder is broken, never forget that the next dumb thing everybody laughs at online could be you.

Smart Tech, Dumb Crime

FOOLED BY FIND MY IPHONE

When a shop clerk in New York City was robbed at gunpoint for her iPhone early last year, a nearby officer knew to spring into action with his own phone. Using the Find My iPhone app, he entered the victim's Apple ID and located the missing mobile in seconds. Wasting no time, he drove over and immediately caught the perp—who'd stashed the pricey device in his sock.

—SOURCE: *NEW YORK DAILY NEWS*

SNAGGED BY SELFIES

Shortly after a victim noticed her iPad had been lifted while she was shopping at a Southern California Costco, she spent some time scrolling through photos on her phone. Lo and behold, snapshots of the alleged thieves were popping up on her iCloud account thanks to the iPad's auto-upload feature. Police released the self-styled mug shots, and the tablet was quickly returned. Maybe the thieves should try Snapchat next time?

—SOURCE: *NEW YORK TIMES*

ID'D BY INSTAGRAM

Nathaniel Troy Maye, 44, and Tiwanna Tenise Thomason, 40, were wanted for identity theft and were caught thanks to some boneheaded social networking. While out for a fancy steak dinner, the couple snapped an Instagram pic and tagged the location. The picture was used in court to help identify the two, who face up to 12 years behind bars. Hashtag #lastmeal?

—SOURCE: *LOS ANGELES TIMES*

SELLING A STEAL ON EBAY

EBay makes selling old junk a snap, but one thief in the Chicago suburbs quickly found that it's not the best place to unload stolen bikes. One victim hopped onto the online auction house after his bike went missing, noticed that it was for sale, and notified police. Detectives won the auction and arrested the suspect upon delivery.

—SOURCE: *CHICAGO TRIBUNE*

Epic Tech Fails 153

It can be surprising to learn the dumb things that happen with smart devices. ***Reader's Digest*** **collected a few of these epic tech fails:**

- ### *The scooter that just didn't catch on*

  The Segway may have debuted to great fanfare (Steve Jobs predicted it would be "as big a deal as the PC"), but this self-balancing electric scooter is now considered little more than a novelty. You may see tourists zipping around on them in major cities, but sales never took off. To compound the sting of Segway's lackluster performance, in 2010, James W. Heselden, the British businessman who owned Segway, fell to his death from a cliff when his scooter malfunctioned during a tour of his estate.

- ### *The tweet that rocked the stock market*

  In April, a false tweet posted on the Twitter account run by the *Associated Press* sent stock markets plummeting within seconds. Hackers had taken over the newswire's official account and tweeted a claim that the White House had been bombed and the president had been injured. While the tweet was stylistically suspicious—the AP would never refer to the president as simply "Barack Obama," and the agency usually writes Breaking to announce a developing story—it still incited market panic: The Dow dropped over 140 points, but it quickly recovered after the AP addressed the hacking.

The device that forgot it had only one job

In the days after a power outage delayed Super Bowl XLVII and shocked viewers, wild rumors circulated about the cause of the blackout. Had Beyoncé's megawatt performance overloaded the system? Was it some kind of cyberattack? The culprit, utility company officials revealed, was actually a device that had recently been put in place to prevent such an outage. Known as a relay, the device had been installed as part of a major upgrade to the Superdome's electrical system in anticipation of the big game. Whether the relay itself was faulty or if user error had caused the device to fail is still in contention.

The app that stranded travelers in the outback

While Apple's infamously unreliable Maps app has been merely a nuisance for most users, it was downright dangerous for those who wanted to visit the Australian city of Mildura. A flaw in the app placed the town 40 miles away from its actual location—and within Murray-Sunset National Park, part of the arid Australian outback, where water is scarce and temperatures can exceed 114°F. After local police were called to the park six times to rescue visitors stranded by navigating with the Apple Maps app, they issued a public warning describing the flaw as "potentially life-threatening."

The tablets that just couldn't quit you

In February 2012, Motorola revealed that 100 used Xoom tablets it had provided to the Internet retailer woot.com for resale still contained personal data from the original owners. Because of an error during the refurbishing process, information that normally would have been erased—photographs, documents, and, potentially most troublesome, user names and passwords—had not been deleted from the units. To compensate, Motorola offered affected customers a two-year membership in an identity theft protection service.

Parents have many good reasons for keeping an eye on their children's Facebook accounts, but one is to help them avoid looking really, really dumb. Here are a few gems collected by the good folks at acidcow.com:

- *"It took me ten minutes to remember how to spell water bottel."*

- *"Sometimes, when I close my eyes, I can't see."*

- *"There is no i in happyness."*

- *"It's a good thing Halloween didn't fall on the 13th this year cuz that would be really scary!"*

- *"Does anyone know if the air from a fan can blow away the particles from a wireless signal?"*

- *"Does every religion celebrate Thanksgiving?"*

- *"My heart is pounding like a nail."*

- *"Dear school: why do you excist? Suncerley me."*

- *"Someone just tried to convince me that the sun is a star. The sun is a #$% sun."*

Hi-tech automation comes to every job, and for those who fly planes it's no different. With remote-controlled drone aircraft now commonplace in the military, aviation officials are already exploring ways to use unmanned planes for routine jobs like flying cargo and policing the skies.

That trend is breathing new life into an old flyboy's joke that's been around since the first autopilots became available: "Future planes will have two pilots: a human and a Doberman. The dog's job is to bite the pilot if he tries to touch anything."

—THE DAILYBEAST.COM

If you ever signed up for anything online, you know what a EULA is—short for "End User License Agreement," it's the long, wordy contract thingy you didn't read before you clicked on "agree."

And the reason you didn't read it is because it was, for all practical purposes, unreadable. PayPal's EULA was recently measured at 36,275 words. Apple's 2011 iTunes EULA was 56 pages long. Who's got time to comb through that kind of verbiage? Nobody.

But never forget: as the old saying goes, the large print giveth, and the small print taketh away.

The website Chive.com's EULA once read, "anyone submitting photos to us agrees to name their firstborn son or daughter Leo." More than seven thousand users clicked "agree" to a Gamestation EULA that read, "By placing an order via this Web site . . . you agree to grant us a non-transferable option to claim, for now and for ever more, your immortal soul."

Most of those sorts of things are jokes—but not all. To prove how absurd EULAs are, the company PC Pitstop once buried a clause in their own EULA promising to send a prize, including money to anyone who asked. It took four months and more than three thousand downloads, but somebody finally wrote in to claim the prize.

In return, the customer got a check for $1,000. "At least for one person," the company said, "it really does pay to read EULAs."

Tech Support: Is the light on your modem blinking?

Customer: No.

Tech Support: So, it is solid then?

Customer: Yes. It's solid, then it's off, then it's solid again, then it's off again . . .

—NOTALWAYSRIGHT.COM

It's well known that cats dominate the Internet. At the wildly popular humor site I Can Has Cheezburger, people submit ten times as many funny-cat pictures as funny-dog pictures. The Net is awash in popular feline mascots such as Maru (famous for his love of cardboard boxes), Henri the Existential Cat ("we cannot escape ourselves," he says), and Grumpy Cat (whose name speaks for itself).

Add to that countless cat-goof videos and the ubiquitous jokey pictures called "laugh-out-loud cats" (LOLcats for short), and dogs don't stand a chance. Even such canine stars as Tyson the Skateboarding Bulldog can't come close.

And while there are many theories as to feline dominance—some say they're more expressive, others that they're more interesting—author and cat expert Steve Dale has a much simpler answer. "In the world of cats, there is no dog park," he says. "For cat owners, the dog park is the Internet."

Tech Support: Yes, ma'am, we require a credit card or checking account in order to sign up on our service.

Customer: Well, I saw on the news that I should never give out my credit card information!

Tech Support: Well, ma'am, we have to have a way to bill you.

Customer: No honest company would ask me for my credit card information!

—RINKWORKS.COM

Once wireless Internet accounts became cheap and popular, it didn't take long for people to start trying to log on for free using other people's accounts.

But if you want to send a message to the moochers or noisy neighbors, all you have to do is give your account the right name. That's what will pop up on the screen when they try to log on. OpenSignalMaps, a company that maintains a database of wi-fi network names collected the following: compiled some of their favorites, including:

- *Go Away Don't Steal My Broadband*

- *Stop Mooching Our Internet*

- *Covet not thy neighbour's wi-fi*

- *Thou shalt not steal!*

- *Stop slamming the door!!!*

- *Stop wearing heels!*

- *Stop shouting!*

Customer: Well, I just want to know if I load this disk into my computer, won't other people be able to get into my computer and access everything I have in there?

Tech Support: No, that's not possible.

Customer: You see it on the TV all the time.

—RINKWORKS.COM

A man tells his doctor, "Doc, help me. I'm addicted to Twitter!" The doctor replies, "Sorry, I don't follow you . . ."

—CHRISTINE SCHRUM

With the rise of Twitter has come the rise of the ubiquitous "hashtags" used to label tweets, like #ReadersDigest or #funnystories.

And while the hashtag format is still a novelty for a lot of us, for many young people, it comes as a surprise that the "#" symbol was ever used for anything else.

Reports one music teacher: "I just had a student ask me how to play F hashtag and C hashtag minor. Words fail."

—SOURCE: LAMEBOOK.COM

When your company sends out too many e-mails, there's only one thing to do: send another e-mail to apologize.

"Hey . . . it happens," wrote the tech company Hewlett-Packard to its customers after mistakenly flooding their inboxes. "Oops."

The good news: they at least offered customers a $10 coupon in exchange for the overload. And apologizing by e-mail was probably less annoying than trying to do it in person.

—TGDAILY.COM

Tech Support: Good morning, thank you for calling.

Customer: Hi, I bought a laptop, and I want to get it set up. Can you talk me through it?

Tech Support: Sure, when you turn on the computer you'll be asked to type in the user name you want to use . . .

Customer: I haven't gotten that far yet. How do I open the box?

Tech Support: Really, you want me to talk you through opening the box?

Customer: Yes.

Tech Support: Is this a prank call?

Customer: No . . .

—NOTALWAYSRIGHT.COM

HI-TECH DUMB

Science fiction and online author Cory Doctorow, an editor at the popular website BoingBoing.net, is a true gizmo lover who likes to keep abreast of the latest in technology. He's recently been experimenting with automatic dictation software that turns speech into typewritten words and shared this funny story from his many travels around the globe:

"This morning, while hurrying down the concourse at LaGuardia Airport, I tried to dictate a text message to my Nexus 4 while wheeling my suitcase behind me," Doctorow wrote. "It got the dictation fine, but appended 'kdkdkdkdkdkdkdkd' to the message—this being its interpretation of the sound of my suitcase wheels on the tiles."

—BOINGBOING.NET

About a year ago, I got a call at work from a customer from Roswell, NM," where many conspiracy theorists believe a UFO crashed back in the 1950s.

To break the ice, I jokingly asked if he or any of his neighbors had seen any aliens lately. The guy laughed and proceeded to tell me all about the "crazies" (his word, not mine) who vacation there in hopes of seeing a UFO themselves.

As he talked, I processed his order, and when I finished I asked him for his e-mail address.

That's when I found out that there's more than one kind of crazy in Roswell. "E-mail!" he shouted. "I won't have anything to do with modems of any sort! Don't you know that once you install a modem, the government can look into your computer and watch everything you do? That's why every night before I go to bed, I turn the monitor to the wall."

—RINKWORKS.COM

Maple Island was rocked by news that one of its citizens had been murdered by his estranged wife.

The fact that Maple Island exists online, as part of the virtual role-playing game MapleStory, doesn't make the news any less shocking. When her virtual husband asked for a virtual divorce, the devastated woman, who lives in Japan, used the password of the real-life man who controlled her online ex to kill off his online persona. (Got that?)

"I was suddenly divorced," said the woman, who was arrested on suspicion of illegally accessing a computer and manipulating electronic data. "That made me so angry."

—*READER'S DIGEST*

Question: Who's more popular online, *People* magazine or a puppy in sunglasses?

Answer: If it's the Internet, the animals win. Major media outlets now all have Facebook accounts and Twitter handles, but if you really want to win followers online it's better to be a cute cat or a snake that's escaped from the zoo. The folks at Mashable.com recently found a long list of pets and wild animals with more followers than name-brand media outlets:

- *A sheepdog named Beast had ten-thousand more followers than* Forbes *magazine.*

- *Sockington the Cat had twenty thousand more followers than ESPN.*

- *The Nyan Cat—a cartoon cat who's shaped like a toaster pastry and flies through space—had twenty thousand more followers than MSNBC.*

- *Boo the Pomeranian had one hundred thousand more followers than* People *magazine.*

- *The turtles who lumbered onto a runway at JFK Airport and blocked a takeoff had 1,500 more followers than a local paper, Newsday.*

HI-TECH DUMB

How Not to Text

Mom: Did you text Camille about needing to talk to her about you know what?

Me: I am Camille . . .

Mom: Oh . . .

—WHENPARENTSTEXT.COM

Jason: Be warned, I'm dumping you when I get home tonight.

Jenna: Fine with me, I was just thinking we could use some time apart.

Jason: WTF JENNA??? I got autocorrected. I meant jumping you, not dumping you. And now you're telling me you want to break up?

Jenna: Well this is awkward.

—DAYLOL.COM

"Jets Patriots Jumphead Goes Herey Barllskdjf Fkdasad fg asdf."

—THE TIMES-PICAYUNE

A wife texts her husband on a frosty winter's morning. "Windows frozen!"

Her husband texts back, "Pour lukewarm water over it."

Five minutes later comes her reply: "Computer completely messed up now."

—CATHERIN HISCOX

Wife: I always watch the food channel.

Husband: Why? It doesn't make you any better at cooking.

Wife: Why do you watch porn? It doesn't make you any better in bed.

—SMARTPHOWNED.COM

Josh: Hey sexy.

Anna: Ummm, this is Anna. I'm pretty sure this was meant for Kellie. You know, Kellie, your girlfriend?

Josh: Nope. It was meant for you.

Anna: Well that changes things, doesn't it?

Josh: I won't tell if you don't tell.

Anna: I don't have to tell. Kellie is reading this over my shoulder.

—SOURCE: BUZZFEED.COM

The Vatican made a huge leap into the 21st Century last year when the Pope signed up for a Twitter account.

And while his account—"@pontifex"—now provides a steady stream of Papal news and spiritual advice ("pray for peace!"), fans who sign up to follow Pope Francis shouldn't expect him to return the favor by tuning in to look at pictures of their kids or hear about their parking ticket beefs.

"He won't follow anyone for now," a spokesman said. "He will be followed."

—SOURCE: NYTIMES.COM

Son: Hey mom, how's your new iPhone?

Mom: itsgoodbutIcantfindthespacebar

—SMARTPHOWNED.COM

HI-TECH DUMB

Hi-Tech Customer Service

Calling for information about one of my credit cards, I got the following recorded prompt: "Please enter your account number as it appears on your card or statement."

I did as instructed, and the system said, "Please enter your five digit ZIP code."

After I put that in, I got a third message: "If you would like your information in English, press one."

—MICHELLE GOLF

When Apple launched its voice-activated digital assistant, Siri, the programmers knew they'd have to stay one step ahead of their customers. So they programmed Siri to respond not only to smart questions ("Siri, where's the closest gas station?" "Six blocks east."), but dumb ones too ("Will you talk dirty to me?" "Okay, the carpet needs vacuuming."). According to Beatweek.com, here are some of Siri's more creative responses to entirely predictable questions:

Q: What are you wearing?
Siri: Aluminosilicate glass and stainless steel. Nice, huh?

Q: How much wood could a woodchuck chuck if a woodchuck could chuck wood?
Siri: Forty-two cords, to be exact.

Q: I need to hide a body.
Siri: What kind of places are you looking for? Reservoirs, mines, dumps, swamps?

Q: What should I wear tomorrow?

Siri: What's wrong with what you're wearing now?

Q: I love you, Siri.

Siri: All you need is love. And your iPhone.

Q: How old are you?

Siri: I don't see why that should matter

Q: I think I'm drunk.

Siri: I found two cabs close to you.

"Online-only content is copy-edited, but less reigorously than print content."

—COLUMBIA JOURNALISM REVIEW

As an IT specialist, you learn to adjust your message depending on who you're talking to. That's why I didn't hang up on the person who called and said, "I've just unplugged my monitor in order to clean it without getting shocked. How do I plug it back in?"

About ten different responses flashed through my mind, none of them kind. But the caller was a manager from high up on the food chain, so I knew I needed to control myself.

So I simply said, "Align the pins with the hole, and push it into the socket."

Satisfied, he hung up.

—RINKWORKS.COM

HI-TECH DUMB

A friend of ours was puzzled with the odd messages left on his answering machine. Day after day friends and family would talk and then say, "Beep." He discovered the reason for the joke when he decided to listen to his greeting.

"Hi," it said. "I'm not in right now, so please leave a beep after the message."

—SHEEBA MATHEW

Few could have predicted it, but one of the funniest places on the Internet is the review section of Amazon.com. Turn your sarcasm button on and enjoy these customers as they share their wit and wisdom.

For a miniature desktop that clips to your steering wheel:

- *This has been a total lifesaver. It allows me to prop my sheet music against the wheel, allowing me to play the guitar with both hands while driving.*

- *As a school bus driver I was never able to check my e-mail and update Facebook while at work. Now I am networking more than ever!*

- *Is there any way to turn the driver's airbag off while using the desk as a child changing table? I just don't think it would be safe otherwise.*

For a male hair-removal cream:

- *I survived 3 minutes before I decided to read the instructions.*

- *I could not find anything about this not being for nose or ear hair. I look like I have been put on a sunbed for too long and people keep asking me why I am crying.*

- *Excellent product. Most prisoners confessed within five minutes of the first application. Can recommend.*

For a gallon jug of milk:

- *Why go to my local store and pay $2.99 for a gallon of milk when I can have it overnight delivered for 10 times that price? As a current Pentagon employee, this makes perfect sense to me.*

- *Has anyone else tried pouring this stuff over dry cereal? A-W-E-S-O-M-E!*

- *This product copiously leaks out of my nose whenever I read these reviews.*

Me: Hello, ma'am. I've taken a look at your computer, and we have found liquid inside.

Customer: Yes, I know.

Me: Umm . . . the liquid appears to be biological in origin. Urine.

Customer: Yes, I know.

Me: Unfortunately, we are prohibited from working on computers that have a biological hazard in them. So I will have your computer available for pickup this afternoon.

Customer: So, when will it be fixed?

Me: I do apologize for the inconvenience, but we are unable to work on computers with this type of issue due to health regulations.

Customer: This is why I didn't tell you guys that it got p***** on! F*** you! I'm going to talk to your manager and get you fired!

—NOTALWAYSRIGHT.COM

"Pardon me," said the young man. I looked up from behind my desk at the library. "How do I get on the computer?"
   "Just tell us your name and wait," I answered.
   "Okay, it's John," he said, "125 pounds."

—LORI RICHARDSON

HI-TECH DUMB

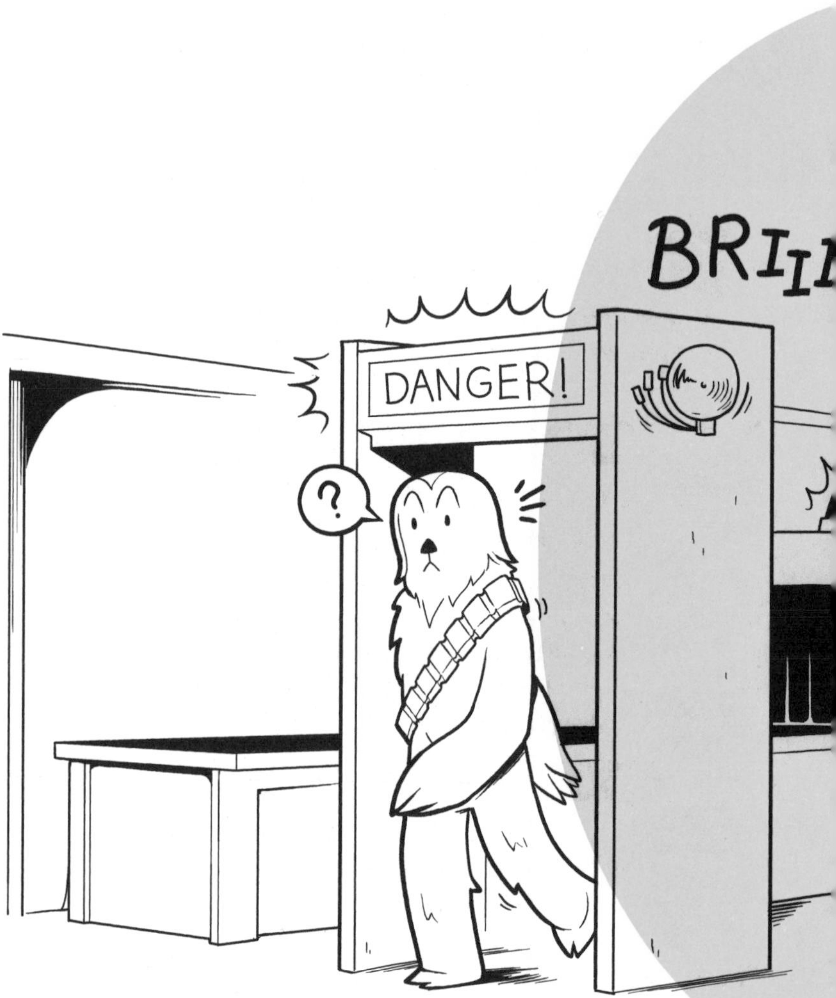

?
DANGER!
BRII

OFFICIALLY
DUMB

THE RED TAPE!
THE TAXES!
THE BUREAUCRACY! THE IDIOCY!

You know it all too well. It's in city hall. It's in Congress. It's in your school board, your town council, and your police department. It's your big dumb government, good people, and it's here to help:

> *Want to bring a plastic light saber or a frosted cupcake on a plane? Too bad—the TSA classifies both as weapons.*

> *Want to pull a rabbit out of a hat? Too bad—you'll need a 30-page bunny evacuation plan first.*

> *Want to look up a word in your elementary school classroom? Too bad—the school board banned the dictionary.*

There is nothing so dumb that some officials somewhere won't think it's a good idea—and there's no good idea they can't turn into something dumb. They'll start with a reasonable concept, like requiring a permit to dam up a creek. But turn your back for five minutes, and next thing you know they're sending cease and desist letters to beavers.

And if there's anything dumber than the people who govern us, it's the election process we use to pick them. As Fox News' Shep Smith once said: "Politics is weird. And creepy. And now I know lacks even the loosest attachment to anything like reality."

It leaves us all wondering at one time or another: Why do we do this to ourselves? Why do we hold these stupid contests to pick these stupid people to create these stupid rules?

The answer, sadly, is that as dumb as our governments may seem to be, we, the governed, are just as dumb.

Yes, it's dumb that you can't bring a nail clipper on a plane. But how dumb is it that every week airport officials catch dozens of Americans trying to bring *loaded weapons* onto planes? It's not like the rules are secret. Bringing a gun on a plane is stupid.

But we just can't stop doing it, just like we can't stop doing the ten thousand other foolish things we do every day.

And that's the root of so much government stupidity: officials have to come up with rules and policies that work for everyone, not just the smart people.

The intentions are usually good. But from the highest offices in Washington to the smallest town councils, officials are human too. It's not that they're trying to be dumb—they just end up looking that way because of their blind adherence to rules, panicky overreaction to threats, or desperate attempts to stay in power.

That can lead to some pretty ugly stuff–and some pretty funny stuff too. So as you enjoy these tales of our dumb elected officials, remember that what you're doing is good for democracy. When the government hears you laughing, it knows you're watching.

The Road to Stupidity Is Paved with Good Intentions

Science can be a crime. That's what Kiera Wilmot found out when she mixed toilet bowl cleaner and aluminum foil in a plastic bottle at her high school in the town of Bartow, Florida. Expecting some smoke, the aspiring chemist found to her surprise that the combination produced a small "bang."

It also produced another unexpected result: she was handcuffed, arrested on felony weapons charges, expelled from school and sent to the local juvenile assessment center.

Wilmot's case drew national attention, and while the school held its ground for a few days, a barrage of online petitions and national coverage changed their tune.

In the end, not only were the charges against Wilmot dropped, but supporters also raised thousands of dollars to send her to a University of Alabama space camp.

—BOINGBOING.NET

Everyone's familiar with the hyper-protective school boards that ban books because of sexy scenes or controversial language. But few can match the visionary leaders of the Menifee Union School District in California, who decided that the best way to handle certain words was to ban the dictionary.

Following a parent's complaint, the sharp-eyed administrators discovered that the Merriam-Webster dictionaries used in elementary classrooms contained a definition for "oral sex." That was enough to trigger the ban, but school officials promised they'd keep looking for more dirt: "It's hard to sit and read the dictionary, but we'll be looking to find other things of a graphic nature," a district spokesperson said.

Fortunately, good sense prevailed, and a district committee reversed the ban. However, the district has promised to provide "alternate dictionaries" for the children of any parents who find Merriam-Webster a bit too racy.

—SOURCE: THEGUARDIAN.COM

If you think there's anything new about trivial, fluff-stuffed political campaigns, consider the experience of the late Dr. Barry Commoner, a pioneering ecologist who ran for president in 1980.

Commoner wanted to make environmental concerns an issue in the race but had little luck. "The peak of the campaign happened in Albuquerque," he later recalled, "where a local reporter said to me, 'Dr. Commoner, are you a serious candidate or are you just running on the issues?'"

—SOURCE: NYTIMES.COM

"Missippi's Literacy Program Shows Improvement."

—ASSOCIATED PRESS

You've heard about Seal Team Six? Well, meet Fawn Team Thirteen. That's how many armed government agents it took to take down a baby deer that was living in an animal shelter in Wisconsin.

The fawn—chillingly dubbed Giggles—was orphaned and brought to the shelter by a worried family. Shelter managers planned to transfer it to a wildlife preserve, but before they could, someone reported them for illegally housing a wild animal.

In response, state wildlife officials staked out the shelter, documented the deer's habits with aerial photographs, presented a detailed case to a judge, and obtained a warrant authorizing a

OFFICIALLY DUMB

covert operation to capture and eliminate the dangerous beast.

That led to a daring daytime raid, in which nine state wildlife officials and four sheriff's deputies—all "armed to the teeth," according to witnesses—surprised the shelter workers, corralled them in a corner, surrounded Giggles's hideout (known to locals as "the barn"), and, after a short but no doubt terrifying battle, brought the doomed fawn out in a body bag.

"That's our policy," one agent told a worker as agents carried Giggles away.

"That's a hell of a policy," the worker replied.

Government officials could have called ahead and asked them about the fawn, but apparently the situation was much too dangerous. "If a sheriff's department is going in to do a search warrant on a drug bust, they don't call them and ask them to voluntarily surrender their marijuana," an official said.

But Wisconsin governor Scott Walker felt differently, ordering officials to review their procedures: "I don't ever want to see something like that again," he said.

—WAUSAUDAILYHERALD.COM

Florida governor Rick Scott meant well. According to *Reuters,* he wanted to give state residents a hotline for information about an outbreak of deadly meningitis.

But instead of reliable public health information, callers heard a sultry woman's voice: "Hello, boys."

Turns out Scott had given out the number for a phone sex business. He wasn't the first to make that kind of mistake, either; according to the Huffington Post, a Wisconsin state senator once miswrote his office number in a newsletter that sent voters to an adult chat line. Not everyone supports that kind of constituent service, but it's sure to win at least a few votes.

Reporter's Notebook

"I was panicked a bit because I really don't know about the Cuban Missile Crisis. It had to do with Cuba and missiles, I'm pretty sure."

—FORMER WHITE HOUSE PRESS SECRETARY DANA PERINO, EXPLAINING
AN ANSWER SHE GAVE ON THE SUBJECT IN A PRESS CONFERENCE

"John, I don't think we pick who we room with here."

—DEMOCRAT BILL DEWEESE TO REPUBLICAN JOHN PERZEL, AFTER THEY BECAME
CELL MATES IN STATE PRISON. ONCE FIERCE RIVALS,
THE PENNSYLVANIA LEGISLATORS WERE BOTH BUSTED FOR CORRUPTION

"Let me be perfectly 'frank.' This is one of my favorite traditions.
I 'relish' it so much . . . who wrote this @#$%?"

—NEW YORK CITY MAYOR MICHAEL BLOOMBERG,
READING A JUNIOR SPEECHWRITER'S BAD PUNS
FOR A CONEY ISLAND HOT–DOG EATING CONTEST

"We just had to use whatever heads we had lying around."

—THE CREATORS OF HBO'S SERIES *GAME OF THRONES,*
WHICH USED A LIKENESS OF GEORGE W. BUSH FOR A SCENE
THAT FEATURED A NUMBER OF SEVERED HEADS ON SPIKES

"You also left me a really good TV sports package. I use it."

—PRESIDENT BARACK OBAMA,
THANKING HIS PREDECESSOR, GEORGE W. BUSH

"I stand by what I said, whatever it was."

—PRESIDENTIAL CANDIDATE MITT ROMNEY,
EXPLAINING A PREVIOUS QUOTE ON A CONTROVERSIAL ISSUE

"I keep hearing about Tumblr. Whatever that is, please use it too."

—OBAMA CAMPAIGN OFFICIAL STEPHANIE CUTTER,
GIVING GUIDANCE TO SUPPORTERS

OFFICIALLY DUMB

When Smart People Turn Dumb

I sold an item through eBay but it got lost in the mail. So I stopped by my local post office and asked them to track it down. "It's not that simple," the clerk scolded. "You have to fill out a mail-loss form before we can initiate a search." "Okay," I said. "I'll take one."

He rummaged under his counter, then went to some other clerks who did the same—only to return and confess, "You'll have to come back later. We can't find the forms."

—DOREEN L. ROGERS

The city of Cedar Rapids, Iowa, wanted a smartphone app that would allow citizens to easily report trash piles and other civic eyesores. But they got more laughs than they bargained for when they called it the "CR App."

To their credit, officials stuck with the name despite the good-natured ribbing—any publicity is good publicity, and the new crap-app was quickly downloaded by more than one thousand users. "We have no intention of changing the name of the app," a spokesperson said. "If the nickname gets more people to download and use it, that's great."

SOURCE: *CEDAR RAPIDS GAZETTE*

Thomas Tolbert of New Mexico was convinced that elections are riddled with fraud, and he set out to prove it by registering his dog to vote. Tolbert used a fake social security number to sign up his black lab, and soon got a registration card in the mail for "Buddy" Tolbert. But after he went on TV to tell the story, election officials announced they were investigating him for voter fraud. Tolbert says he just wanted to show how weak the system is, and he certainly found a weak spot.

—SOURCE: THESMOKINGGUN.COM

Do you remember what happened November 4, 2008? Took out the trash. Walked the dog. Voted for the 44th President of the United States.

That last one was pretty big news to a lot of people, but not to the publisher of the *Sapulpa* (Oklahoma) *Daily Herald*. His paper made no mention of the election in its November 5 edition, other than to note that John McCain won the county.

His rationale? The paper is focused on local news, he said. Of his readers and the elections? "I'm sure they watched it on TV."

—*READER'S DIGEST*

Marty Hahne—a.k.a. Marty the Magician—had just finished his show at a library in Missouri when a mysterious figure emerged from the crowd. "Show me your license," the stranger said.

"License for . . . ? asked the surprised entertainer.

"For the rabbit," said the stranger who was from the Department of Agriculture, enforcing a new regulation requiring Hahne to provide a "disaster plan" to protect his three-pound Netherland Dwarf rabbit from fires, floods, air-conditioning failures, and other acts of God or the electric company.

Hahne had no choice but to comply. He already had the proper rabbit license. But now he also has a 28-page disaster plan and he must also submit a detailed itinerary any time he travels with the rabbit.

All of this springs from a set of laws designed to protect circus animals and other hard-working, often-abused beasts. The real irony is that if Hahne would just periodically eat his rabbits, he wouldn't need any paperwork at all—animals raised as food are exempt from such rules. "I can kill the rabbit right in front of you," Hahne said. "But I can't take it across the street to the birthday party."

—JONATHANTURLEY.COM

OFFICIALLY DUMB

"City Unsure Why the Sewer Smells"

—SOUTH HAVEN TRIBUNE

During the 1974 congressional race, a new candidate was challenging the incumbent in our Iowa district. One of the party loyalists took him to a meeting of farmers.

At the proper time, the loyalist read off the new candidate's qualifications—native Iowan, graduate of an Ivy League college, successful businessman, State Department staffer, member of the U.S. team in crucial negotiations with the Soviet Union, and on and on.

One older farmer who had remained silent through the whole presentation finally indicated that he'd like to talk. Without rising, he stated directly without emotion: "Seems to me it would be a mistake to send this man to Washington."

And then after pausing, he added: "We ought to keep him around for breeding purposes."

—MARTHA PINDER

Many Texas legislators consider it a good thing that their state is far and away the nation's most aggressive user of the death penalty.

In fact, for some, the problem is that the system is entirely too merciful.

That's why they've chosen to eliminate the traditional "last meal" for the condemned. "It is extremely inappropriate," said State Senator John Whitmire, "to give a person sentenced to death such a privilege. Enough is enough."

What triggered this sudden reversal of a centuries-old tradition?

It appears to have been the cheek of convicted murderer Lawrence Russell Brewer, whose last meal request included two chicken-fried steaks, a triple-meat bacon cheeseburger, a cheese omelet, a pound of barbecue, a half-loaf of bread, a meat-lover's pizza, an order of fajitas, fried okra with ketchup, a hunk of peanut butter fudge, a pint of Blue Bell ice cream, and three root beers.

The punch line: Brewer didn't eat any of it. That final poke in the system's eye reportedly infuriated Whitmire. "He wasted a lot of food and a lot of money," the legislator said angrily.

Condemned inmates will now receive the same meals as everyone else, even on their last day above ground. "Sure," said one wit, "leave it to one guy to screw it up for everyone else."

—SOURCE: THEGUARDIAN.COM

When Michigan officials say, "No building without a permit," that's exactly what they mean—and they don't care who you are.

That's what Stephen Tvedten found out when he saw a letter from state officials demanding that he "cease and desist" the construction of two dams on his property.

Trouble was, it wasn't Tvedten building the dams—it was a family of beavers.

Fortunately, the state dropped its concerns once an investigator examined the situation more closely. "It probably would have been a good idea to do the inspection before we sent the notice," one official said.

—SOURCE: SNOPES.COM

Reporter's Notebook II

"No shame in my game. I've sent that out to other women, sure."

—WADE MCCREE, A MICHIGAN JUDGE WHO SENT A SHIRTLESS PICTURE OF HIMSELF
TO A FEMALE BAILIFF, WHOSE HUSBAND WAS NOT AMUSED

"Every citizen has a right to tell their elected officials to go fornicate themselves."

—JIM KENNEY, A PHILADELPHIA CITY COUNCILMAN, IN A TESTY TWITTER
SPAT WITH A LOCAL CONSTITUENT KNOWN AS "THE MOLEMAN"

"The first lesson you learn as a pollster is that people are stupid."

—POLLSTER TOM JENSEN

"We were dead in the water until Victoria's Secret showed up."

—CAPTAIN BRENDAN GENDRON OF THE NEW YORK NATIONAL GUARD, WHOSE
ELECTRIC GENERATORS DIED DURING HURRICANE SANDY. THE LINGERIE COMPANY
DONATED EIGHT LARGE GENERATORS IT HAD STORED NEARBY
FOR AN UPCOMING FASHION SHOW; WIRED.COM

"It was certainly spectacular, but not the way we intended."

—SANDY PURDON, PRODUCER OF SAN DIEGO'S ANNUAL FIREWORKS SHOW, AFTER
SIXTEEN MINUTES' WORTH OF FIREWORKS ACCIDENTALLY WENT OFF IN THIRTY SECONDS

"If somebody's dumb enough to ask me to go to a political convention and say something, they're gonna have to take what they get."

—CLINT EASTWOOD, AFTER MAKING HEADLINES FOR STAGING A SOLILOQUY WITH
AN EMPTY CHAIR AT THE 2012 REPUBLICAN NATIONAL CONVENTION

"Reporters Return to Tibet after Rioting"

—*DAILY CAMERA* (BOULDER, CO)

Does anybody care about spelling anymore? In Virginia, almost 1,500 students at a state university recently received diplomas from the "State of Virgina." (The same diploma misspelled the word *thereto* as *therto*.) Officials apologized and blamed a software upgrade.

On the other hand, with so much to print for so many, it's not surprising that the occasional typo slips past government copy editors. Some recent notables:

● *In Pennsylvania, one of the highway signs for the town of "Ephrata" read "Epharta." Fixing it would cost about $3,000—so it stayed up.*

—SOURCE: FOX NEWS

● *A sign outside a preschool in California reads, "Please Slow Drively." Said one local child, "Maybe it was made by preschoolers."*

— SOURCE: GAWKER

● *A highway sign in Florida misspelled the state name not once, but twice: "Unive of North Flordia—Flordia State College."*

—SOURCE: WOKV.COM

● *The city of South Bend, Indiana, famously promoted its educational excellence with a billboard extolling the "best things about our pubic schools."*

—SOURCE: *THE GUARDIAN*

OFFICIALLY DUMB

- *A traveler in the northern Chicago suburbs spotted signs for "North Chicago Navel Station" and "Campbell Reginal Airport."*

  —SOURCE: LIZARDPRINCESSBEADS.BLOGSPOT.COM

- *One street in New York City warned motorists: "Shcool Xing."*

  —THE GUARDIAN

- *According to its cover, the 2012 directory for congressional staffers was produced by the "Senate Office of Education and Traiing." Proofreading courses were advertised on page 13.*

  —SOURCE: THE GUARDIAN

Airport Security Gone Wrong

Is there any agency that draws more accusations of institutional stupidity than the Transportation Security Administration? Created in the wake of 9/11, it was perhaps inevitable that the agency should become fertile new ground for dumb. It has everything a government bureaucracy needs to be really, really annoying, including:

- *A fundamentally intrusive mission that requires agents to invade your privacy*

- *An inescapable position parked in between you and what you want*

- *An ever-changing list of rules and regulations that frequently confuse even its own employees*

- *Machines that let agents look at you naked*

- *Cells to lock you in if you make a fuss*

All this combined means that in the years since it was founded, TSA agents have been accused of stealing money, groping privates, harassing toddlers and the elderly, breaking medical devices, leaving nasty notes in luggage, pestering travelers about breast milk and prosthetic limbs—the list goes on and on and leads to headlines like:

- *TSA Searches Body-Casted Three-Year-Old in a Wheelchair*
  —SOURCE: BOINGBOING.NET

- *"Family Misses Flight after TSA Gives Pat-Down to Girl with Cerebral Palsy*
  —SOURCE: WASHINGTON.CBSLOCAL.COM

- *Mom with Breast Pump Humiliated by TSA*
  —SOURCE:ABCNEWS.GO.COM

- *Exclusive: TSA Frisks Groom Children to Cooperate with Sex Predators, Abuse Expert Says*
  —SOURCE:RAWSTORY.COM

However, for all their missteps, they still catch a lot of stuff that shouldn't be anywhere near a plane. In one recent week alone, the TSA discovered 49 firearms (36 loaded), 8 stun guns,4 fake grenades, a key ring shaped like a detonator, a cane sword, a lipstick knife, various blades and pointy devices, and "a gag retirement gift designed to look like an improvised explosive device."

So it looks like the TSA is with us to stay. But as long as it is, we'll get stories of bureaucratic bungles like these:

● *Screeners at Newark Airport checked two parents through security and watched them disappear into the crowd—and only then remembered that they forgot to screen the baby. They searched the terminal for half an hour before reporting their mistake, which led Port Authority officials to shut everything down, evacuate the terminal, and bring in the bomb-sniffing dogs. No sign of the family was found—if the baby was set to explode, it's still ticking somewhere.*

—SOURCE: NYDAILYNEWS.COM

● *The seven-foot-three-inch actor who played* Chewbacca *in the original* Star Wars *films was forbidden from bringing his lightsaber on a flight to Dallas. The saber is actually a sturdy cane which actor Peter Mayhew needs to walk. TSA agents refused to let him have the saber until he tweeted his story as he sat in a wheelchair at the departure gate; when the embarrassing re-tweets started flying, the agent relented. "Magic words to TSA are not please or "thank you," Mayhew wrote. "It's Twitter."*

—SOURCE: NBCDFW.COM

● *TSA agents in Las Vegas confiscated a cupcake in a jar because it was partially frosted with what they called a "gel"—and while frosting is permitted, "gels," of course, are forbidden. "I explained that I'd been allowed to bring cupcakes in jars through Boston with no problem," the cupcake's owner recalled, but the agents said, "If Boston had done their job right in the first place, we wouldn't be having this conversation right now."*

—SOURCE: BOINGBOING.NET

Reporter's Notebook III

"The number of US. citizens who died in terrorist attacks increased by two between 2010 and 2011; overall, a comparable number of Americans are crushed to death by their televisions or furniture each year."

—IMPORTANT NEWS FROM THE GOVERNMENT'S
NATIONAL COUNTERTERRORISM CENTER

"I responded in what I thought was the most truthful, or least untruthful manner."

—JAMES CLAPPER, DIRECTOR OF NATIONAL INTELLIGENCE EXPLAINING
A SOMEWHAT MISLEADING ANSWER TO AN EARLIER QUESTION

"I used to say at meetings, 'The illegal we do immediately; the unconstitutional takes a little longer.'"

—FORMER SECRETARY OF STATE HENRY KISSINGER, IN A 1975
CONVERSATION WITH THREE DIPLOMATS

"I've heard of people being killed playing Ping-Pong—Ping-Pongs are more dangerous than guns."

—TEXAS LEGISLATOR KYLE KACAL, EXPLAINING HIS OPPOSITION TO A BILL
THAT WOULD REQUIRE OWNERS TO SECURE ASSAULT WEAPONS

"It had nothing to do with their voting record . . . it had to do with their inability to work with other members, which some people might refer to as the 'a**hole factor.'"

—LESLIE SHEDD, SPOKESPERSON FOR A GEORGIA CONGRESSWOMAN, ON WHY
SOME YOUNGER COLLEAGUES HAD LOST THEIR COMMITTEE ASSIGNMENTS

"There ought to be a law against what I'm doing."

—SEAN O'BYRNE, A BUSINESS LEADER IN KANSAS CITY, DISCUSSING THE TAX
BREAKS AND OTHER INCENTIVES THAT BUSINESSES GET FROM LOCAL GOVERNMENT

OFFICIALLY DUMB

"Governor: Innocent Man Freed After 18 Years Shows Justice System Works"

—LUBBOCK AVALANCHE-JOURNAL

"**W**e're working hard to reduce the deficit, not expand it . . . Why would we spend countless taxpayer dollars on a Death Star with a fundamental flaw that can be exploited by a one-man starship?"

—THE OBAMA ADMINISTRATION'S OFFICIAL RESPONSE TO AN
ONLINE PETITION REQUESTING THAT IT BUILD A DEATH STAR

"**I** am sorry to disappoint you. However, no program or action in relation to mythical animals is warranted."

—A NEW YORK STATE WILDLIFE OFFICIAL RESPONDING
TO A PROPOSED BAN ONBIGFOOT HUNTING

"**F**ederal law still says marijuana is an illegal drug, so don't break out the Cheetos or Goldfish too quickly."

—COLORADO GOVERNOR JOHN HICKENLOOPER, AFTER VOTERS
IN HIS STATE LEGALIZED RECREATIONAL MARIJUANA USE

"**W**e can hardly sit in judgment of your losing $2 billion. We lose twice that every day in Washington."

—SENATOR JIM DEMINT TO WALL STREET TITAN JAMIE DIMON,
CEO OF JPMORGAN CHASE, WHOSE FIRM WAS FACING
$7 BILLION IN FINES FOR VARIOUS FINANCIAL MISDEEDS

"What's a pretty girl like you doing reading those?"

—NEW YORK CITY COUNCIL CANDIDATE ED HARTZOG, ANSWERING A REPORTER
WHO ASKED ABOUT HIS CAMPAIGN FINANCE REPORTS

"I love the fact that the guy is rich."

—PRESIDENTIAL CANDIDATE HERMAN CAIN,
ON HIS FELLOW CANDIDATE MITT ROMNEY

Some headlines demand attention: "California DMV Renews Blind Man's License." The good news is, the man has no intention of driving. Mark Overland is a legally blind lawyer who can see only a small spot directly in front of him—everything else is a blur. He wanted to test the state's ability to weed out people like himself.

So he had his daughter lead him into the testing zone (he decided that using a white cane would be just a little too obvious), where he almost failed because he couldn't find the chart he was supposed to be reading.

But with the help of his daughter and a DMV agent, he found the test and passed it. Two weeks later he got his license in the mail, and publicized his story. Officials had no explanation for the screwup—but they acknowledged that Overland should, in fact, stay off the road. Fortunately, he gave up driving fifteen years ago.

—SOURCE: LATIMES.COM

Try finding work like this in the private sector: "The city of New York is looking to hire someone to encourage breast-feeding in parts of Brooklyn. Annual salary: $73,000."

—SOURCE: GOTHAMIST.COM

OFFICIALLY DUMB

EVERYDAY
DUMB

AND THEN THERE WAS THE DAY YOU SAW THE DUMB THING.

Which day was that?

Here's a hint: it was the day that ended in "y." Here in the golden age of dumb, stupid is as easy to find as fast food. Maybe you heard the one about:

> *The Canadian man who tattooed his brother on a roller coaster. "We've done way more dangerous things, but this is by far the stupidest thing we've ever attempted," said one.*

> *The British store that pulled peanuts off the shelves because they didn't include a label warning customers that the peanuts contained peanuts. "We felt a responsibility to recall the product," a store official said.*

> *The U.S. government agency that won a prize for issuing "a report about reports about reports that recommends the preparation of a report about the report about reports about reports."*

The truth is, even if you don't leave your house, every day will bring its dose of dumb. If you don't see it first hand, you'll hear about it from someone else: a dumb husband story, say. Or a dumb wife story. Or a dumb son or daughter or niece or nephew story. Or a story about dumb blonds, or dumb kids, or dumb retirees, or dumb tourists, or dumb locals, or dumb country folks, or dumb city slickers, or dumb smart people, or dumb dummies, or . . . .

> *Now, waitaminnit. Turns out, that if you listen to us talk about each other, it sounds like we think we're all dumb.*

And maybe we are!

It's not like there's any shortage of evidence. Just look at what we put in our mouths:

A restaurant invents a giant "triple patty" hamburger—and a woman dislocates her jaw trying to take a bite. A Florida pet shop sponsors a roach-eating contest—and a man chokes to death on bug parts. A Texas grill offers a free four-pound steak to anyone who can eat it in an hour—and more than fifty thousand people have tried.

And then there's the couple in Utah who tried to scam a local store by buying its donuts, stuffing them with razor blades–and actually swallowing them.

When we consider the sheer volume of fail tales that come our way every day, it can be hard to believe that such stupidity can be so nakedly displayed.

But part of being dumb is not knowing how dumb you're being. Scientists call it the "Dunning-Kruger effect," named after the researchers at Cornell University whose studies showed that incompetent people are often more confident than their smarter peers.

Why? Put simply, dummies don't know any better. "Not only do these people reach erroneous conclusions and make unfortunate choices," the scientists found, "but their incompetence robs them of the metacognitive ability to realize it."

So always remember: that utterly confident person you're looking at may be a genius—or a total idiot.

But the good news is, just as every day brings its dose of dumb, every day also brings a lesson or two that hopefully leaves us a little smarter. "I like to think of anything stupid I've done as a 'learning experience,'" humorist P. J. O'Rourke says. "It makes me feel less stupid."

Everyday Dumb I

I asked a man on a country road for directions to a friend's house. "Go straight up the road till you reach the place where the barn burned down," he said. "Make a right onto the dirt road till you see a shed with a dog out front, and then make another right, and continue up a mile."

"What if the dog isn't out front?" I asked.

Perplexed, he said, "Make a right, anyway."

—KAREN HENRY

When he was very young, my son was often mistaken for a girl. One day in the park, an elderly woman asked me what his name was.

"James," I replied.

"Jane?" she asked.

"No, James."

"Julie?"

"No, James!" I shouted.

"Oh, James," she said. "Funny name for a girl."

—MANDY BENJAMIN

After a neighbor spotted my father and pregnant mother getting into a car, he rushed over to offer his congratulations. Assuming the man was talking about the car, Dad answered, "Thanks, but it's not mine. It's a friend's."

—JONATHAN TERRY

My mother was reading about immigrants taking the oath of citizenship when she noticed something interesting. "Look at the list of names," she said. "They're all foreigners."

—MARY FRANCES RONDINELLO

In a way, Norm Beamer is just an average American worried about the impact of a big development project proposed for his community by a local fat cat.

But the Palo Alto, California, resident may need a lesson in winning the common man's sympathy.

"It just seems to me that a billionaire can come in and get whatever he wants," Beamer told his local newspaper, "and run roughshod over average millionaires like myself."

—JAY TAYLOR

I visited my daughter bearing gifts: summer squash from my garden.

"What should I do with it?" she asked.

"Whatever you would do with zucchini," I said.

"Okay, we'll give it to our neighbor."

—HAROLD SILVER

When I took my school-age daughters to a lunch with veterans, I told them to ask questions.

One of the men said he'd fought in the Korean War, and the girls were so impressed that the eldest wanted to know more: "Did you fight for the North or the South?"

—LETHA SCRIMPSHER

Most people are smart enough not to wave loaded weapons around in front of the White House.

But Christopher Briggs isn't most people.

Briggs was standing in the street just a few hundred yards from the Oval Office when he started strapping on his .45 caliber pistol. Secret Service agents instantly stopped him and found almost 200 rounds of ammunition in his backpack. Briggs was mystified about his arrest. "I was only going to fire a couple of shots," he said.

—SOURCE: NBCWASHINGTON.COM

EVERYDAY DUMB

If the products we buy are any indication, the human race is doomed.

With a few clicks, any one of us can purchase spray-on hair for our bald spots, a hollow golf club that doubles as a urinal, and special foam for dampening our toilet paper without disintegrating it. There are bras that double as gas masks, dental floss that tastes like bacon, and coffee mugs shaped like toilets (now there's a great way to start the day.)

And while the list of terribly stupid products is almost literally endless, here are a few that deserve special attention:

- *In Puerto Rico, Burger King briefly offered a hands-free hamburger holder. "In a world of multitasking, how can you use your hands to do your daily activities and eat a Whopper at the same time?" the company asked. Surprisingly, it hasn't caught on.*

  —SOURCE: FOXNEWS.COM

- *Following in the footsteps of 7-eleven's "Big Gulp" and other monster-sized drinks, Starbucks, the ubiquitous coffee chain, unveiled the "Trenta." At more than 30 ounces, it holds more liquid than the average human stomach. Starbucks says the Trenta is only for iced drinks, which is a good thing—a Trenta filled with espresso would probably be enough to harm you.*

  —SOURCE: NEWSNATIONALPOST.COM

- *If you ever see someone shrink the more they drink, there may be a simple explanation. The Beerbelly, a "stealth beverage system," is a fake beer gut that allows the wearer to smuggle booze into sporting events, long church sermons, or any other place where openly swigging is frowned upon. Just fill it up, strap it on, and suck on the hidden straw. And don't worry, ladies—for you, the same company makes the WineRack, which hides inside your bra instead of hanging over your belt buckle. "Better than a boob job, and cheaper too," the company says.*

—SOURCE: THE BEERBELLY.COM

● *When kids say a certain toy "stinks," they usually don't mean it literally. But that's not the case with Stinkor, an action figure from Mattel's He-Man series. Stinkor was a skunk-man armed with "he "Stench of Evil," a distinctive foul odor that was actually baked into his plastic body. Stinkor's production run didn't last, but his stink did: 30 years after their brief heyday, Stinkor dolls still smell as bad as the day they were made. "That's what makes him timeless," quipped one aficionado.*

—SOURCE: FASTCODESIGN.COM

● *So you're ready for some exercise, but you face a conundrum. Jogging on the street is too hard on the knees. Jogging on an indoor treadmill is too boring. The solution? A treadmobile—a treadmill-on-wheels that rolls down the street as you run on it. Don't be surprised if you haven't seen one—it's as ugly as it is absurd. "Riding around your neighborhood on a treadmobile tells your neighbors you've pretty much given up on having any sort of positive public image," noted one reviewer. "It's also freaking hilarious."*

—SOURCE: HUFFINGTON POST

● *In case you doubt that intrusive security screenings are now a permanent part of our lives, check the toy department. Until recently, parents could buy a Playmobil Security Check Point play set for toddlers, featuring uniformed figurines and a mini X-ray machine. Older kids can play with the Spy Gear Security Scanner, a functional metal detector just like the ones at the*

EVERYDAY DUMB

airport. "The box really says it all," one writer noted. "A happy child holding his shirt open for a security officer . . . It's like a Hot Wheels commercial directed by Joseph Stalin."

—SOURCE: CONSUMERIST

"Newsmen Threaten Exposure"
—THE GUILD-REPORTER

Overheard between a couple of friends:

"So you and Bob are going to go fishing this weekend? Did you get your fishing licenses yet?"

"No not yet. I'm pretty nervous about it."

"Why would you be nervous?"

"I'm afraid I'm not going to pass the test!"

—STUPIDCOWORKERS.COM

For several years I traveled the northeast as an HVAC-system salesman, and I learned plenty along the way. One evening I overheard this conversation in a bar in Pennsylvania:

Bartender: . . . so then I found out he was secretly taking pictures of me from the other side of the bar.

Customer: Woah! That's weird!

Bartender: Seriously. And then Mark told me he'd just gotten out of prison for killing somebody.

Customer: What?!

Bartender: I know! It really makes me regret having him do my taxes.

—HANK SCUDDER

With the rise of interest in organic foods and "green" living has come a parallel rise in what critics call "greenwashing"—marketing schemes that try to make typical products look more earth-friendly than they actually are.

That's how we ended up with this slogan on the back of a Lay's potato chip bag: "Made with FARM-GROWN potatoes!"

We've made some remarkable advances in agriculture, but there's still no place to grow potatoes besides the dirt. As one wag put it: "At least the potatoes come from a farm, even if the seeds come from a laboratory."

—ANDREW BLECHMAN

The first time famed televangelist Jimmy Swaggart was caught with a prostitute, he tried to win back his congregation with what sounded like a heartfelt apology: "I have sinned against you, my Lord," he said, "and I would ask that Your Precious Blood would wash and cleanse every stain until it is in the seas of God's forgetfulness, not to be remembered against me anymore."

The second time, when pressed for an explanation, Swaggart wasn't quite so remorseful: "The Lord told me it's flat none of your business."

—WIKIPEDIA.ORG

When customers of a Canadian drugstore chain heard Christmas carols over the loudspeakers, they flooded the home office with complaints.

Why? Because it was the first week of November, and Christmas was almost two months away. As CNN reported, "shoppers weren't quite ready for the season to be jolly"—so Shoppers Drug Mart quickly pulled the carols from all 1,200 stores.

—SOURCE: NEWS.BLOGS.CNN.COM

EVERYDAY DUMB

At the fish hatchery where I work, we have a small display that describes an extinct fish that was called the Michigan grayling. One day, a tourist asked me, "Is the grayling still extinct?"

"Yes sir," I said. "It doesn't exist anymore."

"Any thoughts of bringing it back?" he asked.

"No, I don't think that's possible," I said.

"Why not?"

"Because it's extinct."

"Still?"

"Yes."

Frustrated, he left.

—RINKWORKS.COM

Who knew I lived in such a wild area? Our neighborhood newsletter published this warning: "Bikers and walkers, it is suggested you wear clothing when out after dark."

—DENNIS MULDER

Closed-captioning still needs to iron out some kinks. A local news story regarding school closures declared: "The Cleveland Metropolitan School District is holding a nude conference. It promises to be quite an emotional event."

—LINDA TITERA

A TSA official greeted my fellow veterans and our chaperones when we arrived at the airport. Veterans, he said, could go through one security line and didn't need to take off their shoes, while chaperones had to go through another line and did have to remove their shoes.

"But I'm a veteran and a chaperone," said one guy. "What do I do?"

The official thought about it a minute. "Okay, just take off one shoe."

—ERNEST STADVEC

I had ordered vanity plates to go with my very first car. But instead of getting a pair, as I expected, I thought I'd only been sent a single plate.

But I forged proudly ahead with the installation, and when I finished, my father came outside and asked, "Why'd you put only one on?"

"That's all the state sent me," I replied.

Is that right?" Dad said with a grin. Kneeling down, he undid the screws, slid a fingernail along the edge of the plate, and popped off a second one.

The name on my personal plates? "DITZ E 2."

—MICHELLE APOSTOLUDIAS

People complain that technology has made our young people stupider, but the historical record clearly shows that dumb young'uns predate the Internet by a healthy margin. These excerpts from university students' essays were published by *Wilson Quarterly* magazine in 1983:

- *"Victims of the Black Death grew boobs on their necks. The plague also helped the emergance of the English language as the national language of England, France and Italy."*

- *"The Middle Ages slimpared to a halt. The renasence bolted in from the blue. Life reeked with joy."*

- *"Louis XIV became King of the Sun. He gave the people food and artillery. If he didn't like someone, he sent them to the gallows to row for the rest of their lives."*

EVERYDAY DUMB

Spelling makes a difference. I found I wasn't really interested in a recipe I discovered in our local newspaper after reading "Bigger bowels are recommended if you double this recipe."

—CAROLYN FLYNN

Back when I was in high school, I spent an evening watching the Olympics with a friend and her sister. At one point, the sister asked, "Why aren't rodeos an Olympic sport?"

"Probably because the U.S. is the only country where rodeos take place," I said.

"Nuh-uh," she shot back. "Oklahoma has rodeos too."

—RINKWORKS.COM

The air conditioning in my high school civics class was less than ideal. Everyone who sat in the back of the class would freeze, while everyone in the front would roast.

One day, somebody in the back decided to take a stand. "Mrs. Barnes, it's cold in here," he said. "We need to turn the air off."

Since this was a class that was always ready to argue, someone else said, "Turn it off?"

The first student, clearly on his way to a stellar academic career, retorted, "Yeah, off. O-F."

That's when one of our other geniuses decided to pipe up: "I would have laughed so hard if you had spelled that wrong."

—RINKWORKS.COM

Two born-and-raised New Yorkers take their first trip to the West Coast, arriving in L.A. just in time for a heat wave. "Man, it's hot here," says the first New Yorker. "What do you expect?" says the second. "We're 3,000 miles from the ocean."

—BOB MEYERSON

When I brought my mother-in-law home one afternoon, she discovered that she didn't have the key to her second story apartment.

No problem—I went to the garage, took out the ladder, and climbed up, finding that all the windows were locked.

As I stood there on the ladder, deciding whether to break the window or not, she looked up at me and said, "Too bad the landlady isn't here. She has a key to my apartment, and she could go up and open the window for you."

—RINKWORKS.COM

Today, I ran into an old friend who I hadn't seen in years. She raved about how I hadn't aged a bit, and I was all set to thank her when she said, "But, you know, chubby people age better. FML"

—FMYLIFE.COM

"Quickies: 2 morning anchors pregnant"

—*AKRON BEACON JOURNAL*

I was shopping at our local grocery store when I heard a manager say to a worker, "It's slow; go water the plants outside."

"But it's raining," the worker said.

"Take an umbrella," the boss replied.

—NOTALWAYSWORKING.COM

One day in geometry class, a classmate held up one of our clear plastic protractors, looked through its back side, and said, "Hah! Those stupid people put the numbers on backwards!"

I thought she was kidding. She wasn't.

—RINKWORKS.COM

EVERYDAY DUMB

While it's clear that dumb can be found in all fifty American states, few would dispute that there's something special about Florida. The great Dave Barry, a Florida resident and nationally syndicated humorist, was furious to discover that his home state ranked only 47th in a survey of national intelligence. "How dare they suggest that Florida is more intelligent than three other states?" he wrote. "No way."

After all, this is the state that's home to a tourist attraction called "Hug-an-Alligator." This is the state that accidentally banned computers. It's the state where kids drink hand sanitizer for fun, where swinger's parties turn to drunken brawls, and where a church youth minister got 20 years for planning a kidnapping and fantasizing online about "cooking and eating children."

But perhaps nothing illustrates the state's unique nature than the adventures of Florida Man, the "World's Stupidest Superhero." To see what he's up to, follow him on Twitter (@_FloridaMan), or just read the daily headlines to see for yourself:

- *Florida Man Arrested after Eating Bagful of Weed*

- *Florida Man Arrested for Sitting on Crying Baby's Head*

- *Florida Man to Police: "I Might Be a Little Drunk, but I'm Not A Lot of Drunk"*

- *Florida Man Stops to Help Woman after Motorcycle Crash, Steals Purse*

The road by my house was in bad condition after a rough winter. Every day I dodged potholes on the way to work. So I was relieved to see a construction crew working on the road one morning.

Later, on my way home, I noticed no improvement. But where the construction crew had been working stood a new, bright yellow sign with the words "Rough Road."

—SARAH KRAYBILL LIND

I once heard this conversation between a radio announcer and a paleontologist:

Announcer: So what would happen if you mated the woolly mammoth with, say, an elephant?

Expert: Well in the same way that a horse and a donkey produce a mule, we'd get a sort of half-mammoth.

Announcer: So it'd be like some sort of hairy gorilla?

Expert: Um, well, yes, but elephant-shaped, and with tusks.

—RINKWORKS.COM

Everyday Dumb II

We'll do anything to lose weight—except, apparently, eat less and exercise more. Instead, we go for grapefruit diets, leek diets, cookie diets, baby food diets, cabbage soup diets, and candy diets. We try scrubbing ourselves with special soap, stapling our ears, drinking vinegar, and rolling around on the floor. (Old-time movie star Clara Bow loved that one: "I bet I've rolled 100 miles," she said.)

More recently, a woman in Iowa had to see her physician after swallowing a tapeworm, hoping it would eat what she'd already eaten: "One of the damned dumbest things I've ever heard," said one doctor.

—SOURCE: MEDICALDAILY.COM

I overheard an elderly gentleman tell his friend that he couldn't meet him the next day because he had to go to the hospital for an autopsy. His friend was sympathetic: "I had one of those last year. Luckily, it wasn't serious."

—TRACY MORALEE

Like many people, I have an e-mail box that fills with junk I quickly delete. But this past May, one subject line piqued my interest: "Father's Day deals for the man who gave birth to you."

—ROB MACKEY

"McDonald's Fries the Holy Grail for Potato Farmers."

—ASSOCIATED PRESS

The man sitting next to me on a recent flight was terrified of planes; he couldn't stop shaking. So I suggested he get a Scotch from the flight attendant, which he did, drinking it down in one gulp.

"Can I get another one?" he asked me. I pointed out the button above his head and told him to press it if he wanted another drink.

He promptly stood up, pushed the button, and held his glass underneath it.

—ROBERT NURTON

While taking her driving test, my daughter accidentally put the car into reverse and backed into the building. After collecting himself, the proctor said, "You can go ahead and finish the test if you like. It'll be good practice for the next time."

My daughter was flabbergasted. "Are you saying I've failed?"

—BELINDA STONER

After purchasing lumber, I read the warning on the receipt. It confirmed what I already knew—I was happy to be married. The receipt read: "Handling may cause spinsters."

—DIANE SLAUGHTER

The young father took a seat on the bus next to an elderly man and plopped his one-year-old on his lap, just as the little boy began to cry and fidget.

"That child is spoiled, isn't he?" the old man remarked.

"No," said the dad. "They all smell this way."

—ROBERT HOWE

A waiter at our diner was called over by his customer.

"Can you take this dish back?" the customer asked. "I don't like it."

"I'm sorry. What's wrong with it?" asked the waiter.

"It's the hash browns. They taste like potatoes."

—TIA BALCOM

When my 15-year-old son, Pat, stepped up to the plate during a Colt League baseball game, the young announcer declared, "Now batting, the right fielder, number 12, Pathogen!"

After some confusion in the stands, the announcer came back on over the loudspeaker. "Oh, I get it—Pat Hogan!"

—LINDA HOGAN

While online looking at used dining room sets with my sister, I mentioned how surprised I was that so many of the tables and chairs were green. "You don't see that color too often in dining rooms," I said. With great patience, she explained, "Mint is the condition, not the color."

—JACKIE GRADY

The article I read about gathering down from geese was so interesting, I had to share it with my husband.

"Do you know how to get down from a goose?" I asked.

His answer: "Jump?"

—JOAN C. WILSON

EVERYDAY DUMB

In some parts of the world, parents can only choose baby names from officially approved lists.

Not so here in the Land of Freedom. According to social security records, we name our babies Miracle, Goodness, Pretty, Handsome, Money, Shady, Carrion, Rambo, and Vader. We name our children after places we love, like Las Vegas and Lake Erie. We name them after companies we love, like Disney, Apple, Ikea, and ESPN ("Espin").

Sometimes we cobble together names that are practically poetry. The *Houston Press* looked through court records for just one Texas county and found such remarkable examples as Willie Nelson de Ochoa, Heavenleigh Flores, Charmin Crew, Joey Perfecto, and Chastity Spotts. ("I learned about those in health class," one reporter noted.)

And when we don't find a name we like, we just make one up. The folks at Deadspin.com combed through a survey of names from *Parents* magazine, offering up some of our nation's more inspired choices along with a few editorial comments:

- *Blayde:* "The extra Y in there makes it 10 percent sharper."

- *Brylee:* "Isn't this an ice cream brand?"

- *Fallyn:* "I'd like my daughter to sound like a dystopian young adult novel, please."

- *Izander:* "I'd like my son to sound like a shirt. Can you do that?"

- *Jaydien:* "That i is what sets young Jaydien apart from the mere Jaydens of the world."

- *Julissa:* "It joins the likes of Emichelle, Eliza'Betty, and Jessikate."

- *Luxx:* "Why not add that third x and fulfill her destiny?"

- **Sharpay:** *"This is a character from* High School Musical. *It's also a breed of dog. Why stop there? Name your child Dobyrman."*

- **Sketch:** *"At that point, you're just basically looking around the delivery room, coming up with nouns as names."*

- **Tulsa:** *"If you're gonna name your kid after a place, at least have the common courtesy to name him after a legitimate tourist destination."*

- **Zaiden:** *"It takes Jayden and throws a Z in front, which makes it SO STRONG. I just wanna slap a loincloth on little Zaiden and club dragons with him. Be on the lookout for Drayden, Fayden, Waiden, Strayden, and Klayden."*

When I went back to the medical lab to have some blood drawn, I was greeted with a battery of questions from the technician.

"Has your address changed?" she asked.

"No," I answered.

"Your phone number?"

"No."

"What about your birthday?"

—LEWIS SCHERER, JR.

After an enthusiastic recommendation from my wife, I began listening to the audiobook version of Frank McCourt's *Teacher Man.*

"I love it, but his writing style is so disjointed," I complained. "He refers to characters I don't know and introduces them a half hour later."

My wife was as confused as I was, but I soldiered on, disoriented by the jumpy story line. It wasn't until the end of the book that my dilemma was explained—I had set the iPod to Shuffle.

—NORM SUNSHINE

EVERYDAY DUMB

When our church was honoring veterans, my mother filled out a form to have our father included in the church bulletin.

Under *Veteran,* she wrote Dad's name. Under *Branch Service,* she wrote, "Army, 5th Battalion."

Under *Date/Time of Service,* she wrote, "10:30 a.m., but sometimes we go to the 8 a.m."

We changed that to "World War II."

—KAREN MATHEY SKOPHAMMER

My 18-year-old daughter and I were watching TV when a character with my maiden name—Lester Highsmith—was introduced.

I've never heard my name on TV before," I said.

My daughter was equally surprised. "Your name used to be Lester?"

—CARRIE HIGHSMITH PROPER

When I asked my friend if she was planning to attend church, she just shook her head. "I haven't gone in a long time," she said. "Besides, it's too late for me. I've probably already broken all seven commandments."

—NANDIARA HENTGES

There was a historical marker near our West Virginia home commemorating the Civil War Battle of Blue's Gap. One day when an oncoming bus was taking too wide a turn, my wife swerved our van out of the way, accidentally clipped the sign and broke it.

Wanting to do the right thing, I called the state police to report the damage, but apparently the war is still not over around these parts.

"Who won that battle?" asked the trooper.

"The Union," I replied.

"Well, don't worry about it," he said and hung up.

—TED KALVITIS

Readers of the *Roanoke Times* in Virginia woke one day to find a prominent story about a controversial construction project. Among the concerned neighbors was a pregnant mother worried about "the effect on her unborn child of the sound of jackhammers."

The woman, Mellissa Williamson, was featured in a photograph that clearly showed both her growing belly and her dangling cigarette.

Soon the construction project was forgotten as readers swamped the papers with snarky letters attacking Williamson. "Yeah," wrote one critic, "the noise is what the baby needs to fear."

Williamson was unfazed. "It went in one ear and out the other," she said. What's more, she said, her doctor advised her to keep smoking: "It would be good if I cut back, but if I totally quit, it would not only cause stress on me but it would cause stress on the baby."

"L.A. Chimpanzees Get Pregnant Despite Vasectomies"

—*ASSOCIATED PRESS*

My mother joined a new Weight Watchers group. At the first session, the group leader explained the healthy-eating plans everyone should follow, including drinking six to eight glasses of water a day.

The following week, the leader asked how everyone was getting on. One woman looked rather glum.

When the leader asked why, she replied, "Well, I've done my best to stick to the diet plan, but I've had real difficulty. Try as I might, I just can't drink 68 glasses of water a day. All I can manage is 46."

—GILLIAN FRANCE

EVERYDAY DUMB

Heavy snow had buried my van in our driveway. My husband, Scott, dug around the wheels, rocked the van back and forth, and finally pushed me free.

I was on the road when I heard an odd noise. I got on my cell and called home. "Thank God you answered," I said when Scott picked up. "There's this alarming sound coming under the van. For a moment I thought I was dragging you down the highway."

"And you didn't stop?"

—PAIGE FAIRFIELD

Getting through boot camp left my friend Scott feeling like a pretty big deal. So he got a vanity license plate to show exactly what he thought of himself. The plate reads: IM A STD.

—JENNIFER THIEMANN

As we pulled into the parking lot, we saw a couple of people looking under the hood of their car. Concerned, Mom wondered aloud, "Do you think they have a flat tire?"

—BARBARA HEDDEN

My teenage niece Elizabeth was nervous as she took the wheel for her first driving lesson. As she was pulling out of the parking lot, the instructor said, "Turn left here. And don't forget to let the people behind you know what you're doing."

Elizabeth turned to the students sitting in the back seat and announced, "I'm going left."

—RACHEL NICHOLS

All parents are proud of overachieving children, and one father was no exception. The bumper sticker on his car read "My Kid Made Your License Plate."

—ANTHONY TOBIASZ

My friend was on his way home from work and noticed a woman standing in the parking lot looking very worried. When he asked if all was well, she told him she'd locked her keys in the car and had called her husband some distance away to ask him to bring her the spare set.

On impulse, my friend tried the door and found that it was open. "Oh my God!" said the woman. "Quick, can you lock it again?"

—LESLIE OWENS

As my stint in the Coast Guard came to an end, I applied for a job with U.S. Customs and Border Protection. A customs official came to our Coast Guard station to check me out and interview my boss, a guy who would never win a Mr. Congeniality award. Through paper-thin walls, I heard the customs official ask, "Would you trust Mike to walk into a bank vault lined with money and not take any?"

My boss shot back: "How the hell should I know? I don't work at a bank!"

—MIKE WALL

James Labrecque wasn't about to mess around with unhappy buyers on eBay. As a seller, his written policy was, "What you see is what you get, no returns, and no money back."

That worked quite well until he sold an "empty" safe that turned out to have $26,000 hidden inside.

When Labrecque asked the happy buyer for a share of the cash, all he got in return was a big, fat, "tough luck."

"I feel like the stupidest idiot in the world," Labrecque said later. "That's a chunk of change, you know. That's life-altering money."

And while he would eventually claim that the whole thing was a joke, the buyer of the lucky safe has never confirmed that. So maybe Labrecque was pranked—or maybe he really *is* the stupidest idiot in the world.

—SOURCE: WMCTV.COM

EVERYDAY DUMB

My mother asked me to hand out invitations for my brother's surprise birthday party. That's when I realized he was her favorite twin.

—TERRY SANGSTER

A classified ad for a 1991 Ford Tempo recently caught my eye. The reason the car was for sale: "Mother passed away totally loaded."

—CAROL CARDALL

It may not seem that important to some, but for members of Brooklyn's famous Park Slope Food Co-op, few issues have been more contentious than the question of whether or not to boycott Israeli food in protest of the occupation of the West Bank. A senior Reuters opinion writer was among the attendees at a recent meeting on the subject and shared this string of tweets:

- *"The room is tense with passive aggression. Israeli food referendum dominates. Free Oreos given out, but not free hummus."*

- *"7:31 p.m.: First mention of 'fascist food.'"*

- *"Man gets up, says co-op should ban Israeli food only if it bans American food because of Native American occupation."*

- *"Co-op spending $4,000 to rent high school for Israeli vote. And people say Israeli boycott would be bad for economy."*

- *"Have now moved on to tonight's business: whether to eliminate plastic produce bags at Co-op. No vote tonight. Just discussion."*

- *"Final segment of meeting is time for questions about meeting. Man asks question about whether discussion should be for comments . . . or questions."*

I just did my taxes and I'm getting back $150,000. And people say you can't do your own taxes.

—CHANTEL RAE

My wife is a by-the-recipe baker. But that attention to detail still hasn't made her chocolate chip cookies taste any better.

One day, after the cookies had been in the oven awhile, I smelled a familiar odor. "They're burning," I shouted.

"I know," she said nonchalantly.

"Aren't you going to take them out?"

"No. They still have six minutes."

—WILLIAM MCEWEN

We were shopping for clothes when my 13-year-old daughter spotted a hat with *Guinness* written on it.

She put it on and proclaimed, "Look! I'm a genius!"

—LAURA SANDOVAL

I was sound asleep when the telephone jarred me awake. "Hi!" It was my peppy mother-in-law. She proceeded to rattle on about the busy day she had ahead and all the things that awaited her the rest of the week.

"Mom," I interrupted. "It's five in the morning."

"Really?" she said. "What are you doing up so early?"

—ROSEANNE SORCINELLI

Once I'd finished reviewing my daughter's homework, I gave her an impromptu quiz. "What is a group of whales called?" I asked. "I'll give you a hint—it sounds like something you use to listen to music."

"An iPod?" she guessed.

"Close," I said. "But what I'm thinking of is a little smaller."

"A Shuffle!"

—GARY SELINGER

EVERYDAY DUMB

Overheard at the dinosaur exhibit in Disney's Animal Kingdom park: a confused woman complaining to her friend, "How could they possibly know the names of all those dinosaurs if they died 75 million years ago? And another thing, how do we even know they were called dinosaurs?"

—MEGAN LLOYD

I was driving when I saw the flash of a traffic camera. I figured that my picture had been taken for speeding, even though I knew I wasn't. Just to be sure, I went around the block and passed the same spot, driving even more slowly. But again the camera flashed.

Thinking this was pretty funny, I drove past even slower three more times, laughing as the camera snapped away each time while I drove by it at a snail's pace.

Two weeks later, I got five tickets in the mail for driving without a seat belt.

—ADAM J. SMARGON

Pregnant with my third child I was stricken with a bout of morning sickness and lay down on the livingroom couch to rest.

Just then one of the workmen who was doing repairs in my house walked by and gave me a curious look. "Taking a little break," I explained. "I'm in my first trimester."

"Really?" he said. "What's your major?"

—CARA ANDERSON

I was at our state fair when I overheard a little girl pestering her mother: "I want cotton candy!"

"You can have some cotton candy after you eat something healthy," the mom replied.

"I want cotton candy now!"

"I said no," the mother said. "You're going to have something healthy! How about a corn dog?"

—LAURA CURRAN

The 3-D rerelease of James Cameron's landmark film *Titanic* triggered a wave of media stories about the famous disaster, and Twitter, that reliable dipstick into the human condition, quickly revealed that countless young fans had no idea that the *Titanic* was real:

- *Kakia K: "Sooooo, I didn't know the* Titanic *was a real ship that sank . . . "*

- *Kaula N: "Was the* Titanic *a real boat?"*

- *LInsea J: "Am I the only one who didn't know the* Titanic *is a true story?"*

- *Jodie T: "Like did it really sink?*

- *Nai N: "Guys, the* Titanic *was real! #mindblown."*

- *Mr. Dragon Slayer: "Holy #$% I'm never going on a cruise."*

- *Abby S: "I still don't know if the* Titanic *really happened . . . "*

Most of those unfortunate Twitterers suspended their accounts soon after becoming national laughingstocks. That wasn't enough for some, like podcaster Jeff Bakalar: "They shouldn't be kicked off Twitter—they should be put in jail," he said. "No one that stupid will be able to get through life just on honor."

But at least one *Titanic* fan, an ice cream shop worker named Jess, defended herself. "Just because I didn't know doesn't mean I'm thick," she wrote.

Maybe not—but soon afterward, Jess tweeted: "Just realized I've been walking around with a pen between my boobs for the last hour."

Also Available from Reader's Digest

Laughter, the Best Medicine

More than 600 jokes, gags, and laugh lines. Drawn from one of the most popular features of *Reader's Digest* magazine, this lighthearted collection of jokes, one-liners, and other glimpses of life is just what the doctor ordered.

ISBN 978-0-89577-977-9 • $9.95 paperback

Laughter Really Is the Best Medicine

Guaranteed to put laughter in your day, this side-splitting compilation of jokes pokes fun at the facts and foibles of daily routines. This little volume is sure to tickle your funny bone.

ISBN 978-1-60652-204-2 • $9.95 paperback

Laughter Still Is the Best Medicine

According to doctors and scientific researchers, laughter can reduce stress, lower blood pressure, boost the immune system, and even protect your heart. This hilarious collection offers up some of the funniest moments that get us through our day, with jokes, gags, and cartoons that will have readers laughing out loud.

ISBN 978-1-62145-137-2 • $9.99 paperback

For more information, visit us at RDTradePublishing.com
E-book editions are also available.

Reader's Digest books can be purchased through
retail and online bookstores.